Acknowledgements

We wish to acknowledge the help of the following people:
Gwen Ford, Sarah Oakes, Mark Mulligan, Catherine
Sharkey; Lyn Moffett; Dr Brian Tipping, Research Services
Ireland; Patricia McGrory, Dr John Yarnell, Department
of Public Health Queen's University & The Health
Promotion Agency; Dr Debbie Donnelly, NISRA; John
Park, Social Services Inspectorate; Tony McQuillan,
Northern Ireland Housing Executive; Dr Andrew Finlay,
Trinity College Dublin; The Community Information
Technology Unit, Belfast; Paul O'Connor; Rosemary
McCrindle; Victor Cole; Liza McCormick; Sheila Eillot;
Jason Docherty; Rhona Henderson; Paul Monahan;
Eileen McGonnell; Johnny Nolan; Paula Fearon; Des
Reilly; Roisin Kelly; Susan Ingram; Barry Gormley; Ken
Humes; Janis Quinn; Caral Ni Chuilin; Anthony
McIntyre; Julie Finlay, Brian Cole, Siobhan Maguire,
Olivia Hanna, Andy White, Aidan Molloy, Phyliss
Woods, Leah Wilson, Maura McKendry, Margaret
Scullion, Dermot McMahon, Geoff Wilson and Fred
McIlmoyle. David Clements; Brendan Bradley; John
Millar; Marie McNeice; Hazel McCready; Sandra Peake;
and Sam Malcolmson.

The Board of the Cost of the Troubles Study are:
David Clements; Brendan Bradley; John Millar;
Marie McNeice; Hazel McCready; Sandra Peake;
Sam Malcolmson; Mike Morrissey and Marie Smyth.

Table of contents

Executive summary

Background to the survey

- The Cost of the Troubles Study, a group of people bereaved or injured in the Troubles working with academic researchers, have conducted a survey across Northern Ireland.

Goals and purpose

- The purpose of the survey was to establish the range of experiences people had of the Troubles, and how their experiences had affected them.

- The goal of this survey is to make available to policy makers and service providers a comprehensive picture of the range of issues and needs that are prevalent in sections of the Northern Ireland population as a result of the Troubles

Methods

- To construct a sample, wards in Northern Ireland were divided in to three categories:

    those with a high Troubles-related death rate - high intensity areas (over 7 deaths per thousand population);
    those with a medium death rate (over 1 but under 7 per thousand population) - medium intensity areas; and
    those with a low death rate (under 1 per thousand population) - low intensity areas.

- In-depth interviews with 75 people were conducted in order to provide data on a range of experiences and effects of the Troubles. A questionnaire was designed on the basis of this interview data. A standard health instrument (SF12) was also used in the questionnaire.

- All of those individuals surveyed were first written to, and given an opportunity to refuse to participate. Publicity about the survey was organised so that the public knew who was doing the survey, and what its purpose was.

- 30 interviewers administered the questionnaire to 1,346

people from an attempted sample of 3,000 drawn randomly from the electoral registers of 30 wards.

- Interviewers were trained to give information about support services or make referrals where appropriate when they encountered people in need or distress.

Findings

Socio-economic factors

- Respondents in high intensity areas reported lower incomes, higher occupancy of public sector housing, higher unemployment and more benefit dependency than either of the other two locations.

Experience of the Troubles

- Overall, respondents in high intensity areas reported more experience of the Troubles, followed by those in medium intensity areas. Those in low intensity areas reported least experience overall.

- However, those in high intensity areas, reported less experience of less extreme experiences, such as seeing news broadcasts related to the Troubles, and about the same level as the other two areas of medium range experiences such as getting stopped at a checkpoint.

- For all other intense experiences of the Troubles, those in high intensity areas reported levels of experience far in excess of medium and low intensity areas. For example, 28% of those in high intensity areas reported having their home attacked, and 10% reported having their home destroyed.

Effects of the Troubles

- Over a third of respondents in wards of highest intensity reported painful memories compared to a fifth in the middle intensity group:

- Over a quarter in wards of highest intensity reported dreams and nightmares compared to an eighth in the middle intensity group;

- A third in wards of highest intensity reported involuntary recall compared to an eighth in the middle intensity group;
- 30 per cent in wards of highest intensity felt some form of guilt at surviving compared to 11 per cent in the middle intensity group;
- Almost a quarter in wards of highest intensity had taken some form of medication for such effects compared to just under an eighth in middle intensity wards;
- 22 per cent in wards of highest intensity reported an increase in alcohol consumption related to the Troubles compared to just over four per cent in middle intensity wards;
- those in high intensity wards had more severe experiences and reported more severe effects of the Troubles than those in the other two wards;
- those in high intensity wards also reported more health problems than those in the other two areas.

Help and support with the effects of the Troubles

- Those in high intensity wards sought help more frequently than those in other wards;
- In all cases, help was sought primarily from friends and immediate family although some differences emerged in help sought outside the family between the three locations;
- Those in high intensity areas were less likely to seek help from their minister or priest, solicitor, psychiatrist, counsellor or community nurse than those in the other two areas;
- Over 40 per cent of those who sought help in high intensity wards were unable to find satisfactory help, compared to 29 per cent in medium intensity and 29 per cent in low intensity wards;
- Over 83 per cent in high intensity wards believed that nothing could help them, compared to just over 4 per cent

in medium intensity and just over 12 per cent in low intensity wards;

- Over 23 per cent had taken medication in high intensity wards compared to almost 12 per cent in medium wards and just over 9 per cent in low intensity wards;

- Of those who used medication, over 52 per cent of those in high intensity wards were on medication permanently, compared to 9 per cent in medium intensity and 35 per cent for low intensity wards;

- Those using medication in high intensity wards were likely to be using it for sleep disturbance, sedation or anti-depressive purposes, whereas those in low intensity wards used them for pain control rather than for anti-depressive purposes.

Who do people hold accountable?

- Those in the wards least affected tended to blame Loyalist and Republican paramilitaries for the Troubles, whereas those in the wards most affected tended to blame Loyalist but not Republican paramilitaries and the police and army.

What is the clearest predictor of need?

- Differences between areas were analysed via cross-tabulation. Chi-Square was used as a significance test of these differences. Given the very large number of cross-tabulations generated, difference was tested at the .005 level.

- There is wide variation amongst people in Northern Ireland in terms of both their experience of the Troubles and the effect on them. Above all, location - whether a high, medium or low intensity area is the best predictor of the extent of experience of the Troubles, and of the effect of the Troubles.

- Males were more likely to report being involved in physical fights whereas females reported more disrupted schooling and more often felt blamed for the Troubles.

- Catholics in all three locations had more experience of the Troubles and also reported more effects of the Troubles on them. However, of the three key factors - gender, religion and location - the latter was the most important factor.

In high intensity wards:

1. There is the much greater exposure to Troubles-related events both from paramilitary organisations and the security forces - a set of experiences almost unmatched in the rest of Northern Ireland (this group of wards regularly reported experience of Troubles' related activity at twice the rate for middle wards and four times the rate for least intensity wards);

2. There are insecurities and fears in being outside one's own area and an acute wariness of outsiders, for example reflected in efforts to conceal where one lives;

3. There is a strong pattern of segregation - over a quarter of those from highest intensity wards who were employed, worked only with members of their own community.

Experience and effects of the Troubles

There is no straightforward relationship between individual experience of the Troubles and effects of the Troubles.

- 3.7% of the whole sample reported that they had a lot of experience of the Troubles and that it had completely changed their lives;

- Just over half of those with "a lot" of experience of the Troubles indicated some change in their lives, compared to a fifth who said there had been a complete change.

- Most of those who reported a lot, quite a lot or some, most commonly reported "some" change in their lives

A measure of Post Traumatic Stress

An indicator of post-traumatic stress, loosely based on the diagnostic criteria for Post Traumatic Stress Disorder was constructed and 390 cases, about 30% of the entire sample met the criteria. Only small differences were noted between men and women, but large religious differences emerged, with Catholics reporting more stress than Protestants. Similarly, those living in the highest intensity wards reported more stress than those in medium intensity, and those in low intensity reported less stress than either of the other two cohorts.

Conclusions

Location and religion stand out as significant factors in both the experience and the effects of the Troubles. Other factors such as segregation and levels of deprivation seem to be related to the level of exposure to Troubles related experiences, and the degree of impact of the Troubles on people's lives.

Recommendations

1. The concentration of Troubles-related violence in certain location and sub-sets of the population should be recognised by policy makers and service providers, especially in targeting social need.

2. The role of immediate families in providing support for those affected by the Troubles should be formally recognised and supported by policy makers and service providers;

3. There is a need to learn more about those who have been offering social support to those affected by the Troubles in order to offer support and recognition for work, which has been the major and most effective source of help in this field.

4. Further work is required on the role of prescribed medication and alcohol in the management of Troubles related stress, especially in the light of the poorer overall health reported in the areas worst affected by the Troubles.

Introduction

The survey presented here was conducted in the context of a larger study, implemented according to participative action research principles concerned with establishing the effects of the Northern Ireland "Troubles" on the Northern Ireland population as a whole. The work presented here - a survey of Northern Ireland - is the final research report in a series of reports arising out of the project. This report constitutes a preliminary analysis of the survey data. Further analysis will be undertaken and published as papers in the future.

Background to the work

Early in the Troubles, there was disagreement amongst psychiatrists and psychologists about the effect of the Troubles on section of the population. (No comprehensive study has examined the impact on the population as a whole.) Some, notably Fraser (1971; Fraser et al 1972) maintained that observable effects of exposure to violence had occurred, whilst others such as Lyons (1974) or later Cairns and Wilson (1989) tended to support the view that traumatic symptoms rapidly improved after a violent event and that those exposed to violence of the Troubles coped successfully. Since that early debate, although there has been some investigation of the impact of the Troubles on attitudes and moral development, there has been remarkably little consistent interest in the specific mental health or other effects of the Troubles on the population, nor is there any generally recognised and reliable measure of the general effects of the Troubles on the population of Northern Ireland.[1] It was in this context that the study was established.

In the wake of cease-fires from 1994 onwards, a group of people from all sections of the population in Northern Ireland who had direct experience of being bereaved or injured in the Troubles were brought together to discuss their position and possible contribution to the new political situation. The widespread determination to see a permanent end to violence seemed to be based on the implicit recognition of the damage done by the violence of the Troubles, yet there was no reliable collated evidence of this damage, nor was there documentation of the needs that might have to be met should peace break out. This group formed 'The Cost of the Troubles Study', which became a limited company and a recognised charity. In partnership with academic researchers from the university sector, a study of the effects of the Troubles on the population was planned and initiated.

The research approach

We have documented elsewhere (Smyth & Moore, 1996) concerns about the relationship of researchers to those who participate as "subjects." We wish to resist the practice of using informants or respondents simply as containers of data that must be collected. Our training in research does not necessarily equip us to consider the rights of the respondent, not does it demand that we consider the appropriation of information and the subsequent marginalization of the respondent from the process of analysis as problematic.

Like media coverage, research is usually engaged in the collection of evidence to support or contradict pre-existing ideas about the subject investigated. In neither case does the interviewee or "subject" exert much influence, if any, on the angle of the journalist or the analysis of researcher. Furthermore, having given consent to being interviewed, filmed or otherwise represented, usually the "subject" exerts no further control over the manner in which the footage, sound-track or data is deployed. This material may be used again, usually without consultation with those who generated it, when documentary media material is being compiled, or in further research.

This research is conducted in accordance with participatory action research principles, which have entailed a management

---

[1] Research has been conducted on various sub populations such as children (Cairns, E. Caught in Crossfire: Children and the Northern Ireland Conflict. Belfast, Appletree.), or various groups of people, such as litigants for compensation (Bell, P. Kee, G. Loughrey, R. Roddy, R.J. and Curran, P.S. (1988) "Post-traumatic stress in Northern Ireland." Acta Psychiatr. Scand. 1988: 77: 166-169, or those affected by the Enniskillen bomb of November 1987: Curran, P.S. Bell, P. Murray, A. Loughrey, G. Roddy, R. & Rocke, L.G. (1990) Psychological Consequences of the Enniskillen Bombing. British Journal of Psychiatry (1990) 156: 479-482.

structure involving a range of people with direct experience of the effects of the Troubles. There are ethical considerations related to entering this field of research that confirmed the desirability of this approach. One of the most devastating after-effects of trauma is the sense of disempowerment that it can bring. Working according to a principle of partnership is an attempt to avoid further disempowering those whose lives and experience we set out to research and document. We identified the need to deal responsibly with the vulnerabilities of those whose experiences they seek to portray or understand.

Attempting to democratise the research process, by involving individuals from the researched population was one of the strategies employed in order to attempt to address this issue. The term "participatory action research" has been applied to strategies which attempt to engage the researched population in this way. This approach has been developed in previous work.[2] In this project, it entails, for example, the democratising the management structure of the project management, as described above. The meant the involvement of lay management in monitoring the ethical aspects of research practices; the involvement of lay people in analysis by discussion and by reviewing our findings and analysis; a detailed process of providing transcripts to all interviewees; discussion and agreeing of transcripts; collaboration with interviewees on issues such as anonymity, and presentation of findings.

The structure of the project

The project consists of three groupings: the Board of Directors which is the executive body and the fund-holder; the Board of Directors has legal and executive responsibility for the management of the project. The Board of Directors is composed of many of the people who met after the cease-fires of 1994 and are from both sides of the sectarian divide in Northern Ireland, and all have direct experience of being bereaved or injured in the Troubles. Two of the research team also sit on the Board. The

---

[2] See the work of Templegrove Action Research, for example, (1996) Hemmed In and Hacking It: Word and Images from Two Enclaves in Northern Ireland: Derry Londonderry. Guildhall Press.

advisory group is a non-executive group that meets regularly with the research team, and is composed of funders, policy-makers and experts in the field. The research team is composed of two full and one part-time staff members (two of whom are also directors. The advisory group play a valuable role in reviewing the survey and questionnaire design, and in commenting on some of the analysis. The research team are responsible for conducting the research, and are supported and advised by the advisory group, while retaining professional autonomy on research issues. The structure of the project offers the possibility of incorporating into the research design, management and analysis the perspectives of those in the researched population.

The overall scope of the project

The task of the larger study was to document the effects of the Troubles on the population as a whole, and to elucidate any patterns or trends in the way the effects of the Troubles are distributed within the population. The project employed both qualitative and quantitative methods, and people who have been directly affected by the Troubles informed the direction of the research.

To this end, a tripartite research strategy was employed:

- Phase one of the project identified the full range of self-help groups established by people adversely affected by the violence of the Troubles. A directory of groups and services available to those experiencing physical or emotional after-effects related to the Troubles was drawn up and made available to all interviewers who could then pass it to respondents where appropriate. Phase one also produced a database of deaths in the Troubles from 1969 to date. This database was used to calculate ward death rates, and an analysis of this database has been published separately (Fay, Morrissey and Smyth, 1998) The database had been compiled primarily to provide a framework for stratifying the sample for the survey, and it was also used for this purpose as we will discuss later.

- Phase two involved conducting interviews with

approximately 70 people to generate in-depth accounts for qualitative analysis. These data also informed the design of a questionnaire for use the field survey of a representative sample of 3,000 people drawn from the general population. Arguably, the richest data on the experiences and effects of the Troubles in this project was collected in the in-depth interviews. However, it was anticipated that policy makers and others with a policy eye on these issues, might find a survey which 'tested' the wider validity and reliability of the qualitative data useful. Therefore, qualitative data was collected and, alongside being analysed and presented as qualitative data, it was used to inform the design of a questionnaire. Further information about the qualitative data collection is contained in Appendix 2, and a selection of quotes from the interviews is presented in Appendix 3.

- Phase three consisted of the conduct and analysis of this survey. The aims of the survey are to establish the prevalence of emotional and physical sequelae arising out of the Troubles in Northern Ireland, and to identify the needs (health, emotional, social, financial) of those affected. This involved administering a questionnaire to a representative sample of the population of Northern Ireland. No existing questionnaire was adequate to the task, and it was necessary to develop an instrument for this purpose. We see this as the first of a series of papers and reports on the survey.

Phase three also consisted of the dissemination of the results of all findings of the project.

Objectivity and value-freedom

We have also written earlier (Fay, Morrissey and Smyth: 1998) about the issue of professional value freedom, and described how we decided to depart from the professional norm. The ethical concerns arising out of the claim to value-freedom and objectivity must concern researchers investigating violence and its effects. The idea of conducting a survey conjures up an image of anonymity, answers that can be coded numerically, and the routine collection of data door to door. However, we had to consider what we should do if we uncovered distress or unmet needs. Would we simply record this as data and remain detached, or would we attempt to link the person in need with supportive services? Furthermore, as we had found in working on the database on deaths, daily handling of the tragic and often heartbreaking details of people's lives has a personal impact on the researcher. In earlier stages of the project work, we were constantly reminded of the nature of the data we were handling, and had to deal with our emotional responses. We tried to practice the discipline of remembering that these data represent the suffering and loss of human beings, in the context of a society that often copes with the scale of loss by denying this. Contrary to the old models of scientific or professional distance, and to the silence and denial that is commonly used to cope with the tragedies of the Troubles, we have not denied these responses to each other, - rather, we have discussed our personal responses to the data, and made it part of our interviewer training and support, and ultimately part of our analysis. However, this had implications for the way we set about conducting the survey, as we describe later.

Ethical issues in collecting and analysing data on the Troubles

In the initial stages of the project, we acutely felt the responsibility of holding information on over 3,500 people who had died, and interview material from over 70 people. In relation to the data on deaths in the Troubles, the Board of Directors took the view that, even though some of the personal information on those killed is already in the public arena, (e.g. Sutton, 1994) we would not make available any personal details lest the information be used to invade the privacy of families, or worse, that revenge or other motivations be facilitated.

In relation to the survey, we had anxieties about "cold-calling" at people's homes without warning, so we wrote in advance, informing people that we were intending to call and ask them to complete a questionnaire on their experiences of the Troubles and the effects of the Troubles on them. Our anxiety was that we would invade the privacy of people who had been affected, and cause them distress. When we discuss the response rate to the survey, we will outline the response to our initial letter.

Uncovering need

We also anticipated that we would discover unmet needs or problems that interviewees in both the survey and the in-depth interviews had, and for which they might require help or support. We therefore compiled a list of agencies and their contact details that offered support or help in this field, and drew up a leaflet which could be distributed to those who wished to have a copy. The remainder of the leaflet, was written in collaboration with two women who had been bereaved and injured in the Troubles. They told us of advice that they wished they had had when they were first affected by the Troubles and we used what they said to draw up the leaflet. We also directly referred people to other agencies where they wished us to do so.

Role of research in the wider society

We have been researching at a time of crucial importance to the future of Northern Ireland, and we are conscious of the responsibility we all have to contribute in positive ways to political progress and peace. The information we handle and present here is not objective or neutral. The bare statistics cannot properly represent the pain and suffering of individuals, families and communities. Presenting such facts and figures in the times we are in is a responsibility we feel acutely. We worry that our work will be used in ways that will contribute to the entrenchment of positions, and more bloodshed and loss of life may indirectly result. There is no possible evasion of this responsibility. Yet we must continue to believe that more and better evidence of the awful cost paid by this community will support, inspire and motivate some people to pursue new ways in which we can peacefully and successfully address our situation. Furthermore, we work in hope that our work will inspire those in authority to devote significant resources where they are most needed in order to redress the damage that has been done by almost thirty years of the Troubles.

We continue to research in hope that some of our findings may be useful in shedding light on the legacy of the Troubles, particularly within some of the areas and sub-populations worst affected, and thereby illuminate the routes towards new and effective solutions.

Constructing the Questionnaire

The questionnaire was designed in five parts.

1. Cover sheet and introduction

This first section contained the date of the interview, questionnaire serial number, ward and interviewer codes, to be used for response rate monitoring and quality control purposes. A written introduction to the survey was also provided for the interviewer to read to each interviewee. This introduction set out the purpose of the survey, conditions of confidentiality, distress and arrangements for further support and help if required.

2. Demographics

This section aimed at collecting data on household composition, tenure and type of housing, occupation and work status, benefits and income, and religion and ethnic origin.

3. Health and well being

It was decided that a standardised measure of health should be included in the questionnaire. The General Health Questionnaire was considered, but found to collect little data on emotional and psychological health. For this reason, the Short Form 36 (SF36) was considered, since it contained a wider range of data. However, the SF36 comprised 36 questions overall, and since the questionnaire was already lengthy, this was considered a problem. When it was discovered that a shorter version of the SF36 was available, - the SF12, comprising only 12 questions, it was decided to use this instrument. However, one question, shown as Question 33 in the final questionnaire had to be altered to take account of language and cultural differences. The original SF12 question reads, "Have you felt downhearted and blue?" The word "blue" was altered to "depressed." A further question, Question 36 in the final questionnaire, was added to this section, asking respondents to identify causes, including Troubles-related causes, for changes in their health.

4. Experience of the Troubles

This section and the following section were designed as a result of the analysis of the qualitative data. It was necessary, when analysing the qualitative data to organise it into categories, and a coding tree was devised by which the interview transcripts were coded, and these formed the basis for the main section in the questionnaire. The main sections on this tree were as follows:

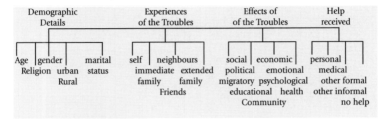

At a later stage in the qualitative analysis, other nodes were added to the tree, (nodes 5 onwards - see Appendix 3 for a full list of nodes) but for the purposes of the questionnaire design, the branches illustrated are the key categories that went to form the design of the questionnaire. The two key areas of enquiry are:

(a) experiences of the Troubles and
(b) effects of the Troubles.

Using the data collected in interviews, we ordered questions in the questionnaire, so that they began with relatively common and less distressing experiences of the Troubles and escalated gradually to the more severe and distressing experiences, thus:

* Common experiences
* More direct experiences
* Work experiences/intimidation
* Severe experiences
* Injury or death in the Troubles

To this section we added questions on three other issues:

* Responsibility for Troubles
* Time periods of the Troubles affecting you
* Specific events affecting you

We used issues and comments that had recurred in the interviews to inform the design of the questions on experience of the Troubles.

Similarly, the section on effects of the Troubles was partly informed by data collected in interviews with the exception of the first two sections, Post Traumatic Stress Disorder symptoms and recency, onset and disruption to life caused by these symptoms. The complete contents of this section is shown below:

5. **Effects of Troubles on you**
    *   PTSD symptoms
    *   Recency, onset and disruption to life
    *   Medication & self medication
    *   Effect on health
    *   Effect on family
    *   Effect on education, work, income
    *   Effect on leisure
    *   Effect on moral attitudes
    *   Effect on political attitudes
    *   Effect on attitude to law and order
    *   Degree of effect
    *   Access to and use of help and support
    *   Compensation
    *   Legal redress

Again, questions were worded to reflect the range of responses that we had encountered in the interview data. A draft questionnaire was designed, and circulated to the advisory group, the Board of Directors and other interested parties for comment. The draft design was amended after each set of suggestions from one source and re-circulated. This process was repeated each time substantial amendments were made. Whilst time consuming and at times frustrating, after approximately 12 drafts, a final version was agreed for piloting.

Field-force, recruitment, training, debriefing

The administration of the questionnaire was subcontracted, although the research team were involved in setting criteria for recruitment of the fieldforce. The posts for interviewers were advertised in local Training and Employment Agencies and universities. Successful applicants were required to have previous experiences in administering questionnaires, the ability to record information clearly and accurately, the ability to deal sympathetically and sensitively with interviewees and an understanding of the importance of confidentiality. Advertisements for posts stated that it was desirable but not essential for candidates to have a university degree. In the main, interviewers were graduates, and if possible local graduates from the wards they were interviewing in. In all, thirty-one interviewers were selected and trained. Interviewers were provided with training from the research team on the ethical issues involved in the fieldwork, and the range of response likely to be encountered in interviews, as well as training in interview techniques questionnaire administration. The research team also provided debriefing sessions for interviewers, and were available to take referrals from them, should the need arise to make a referral to a supportive service. The fieldforce were also piloted alongside the questionnaire.

Piloting the questionnaire

The questionnaire was piloted alongside the fieldforce. Each interviewer was given four questionnaires and the names and addresses of four interviewees in the ward he or she was to work in during the main survey. Interviewees were selected according to the procedure used to draw the main sample, namely, random numbers were generated and the interviewees were selected from the electoral list according to the list of random numbers.

Several things emerged from the pilot. First, the questionnaire required only minor adjustments to instructions to answer questions, and the wording in one or two questions. These adjustments were made. Second, the fieldforce required instruction to fill in all answers, not just the positive responses. Third, the electoral list, which was the most recent list at the time of the survey, seemed to have a large number of registered electors who were not at the listed address. The response rate was low, partly due to the large number of such erroneous listings, and partly due to other factors that were not entirely clear. These factors may include the subject area of the survey, and reticence on the part of some interviewees to answer questions about a sensitive subject, such as the Troubles. The necessary amendments were made to the questionnaire, and a copy of the final questionnaire is included as Appendix 1. Further briefings were given to the fieldforce on question completion, and on handling the issues surrounding the response rate. The difficulties with the electoral list were beyond our control, but we did decide to embark on a vigorous publicity campaign on the survey, in order to maximise the response rate, and lower levels of suspicion in certain wards.

An earlier discussion had taken place about the advisability of using a financial incentive to increase the response rate, but our Board of Directors felt that this was inappropriate given the nature of the survey. Instead, we prepared information leaflets on the survey and on the Cost of the Troubles Study and conducted a mail-shot of over 400 community groups throughout Northern Ireland, through the use of Northern Ireland Council for Voluntary Action's circulation of Scope magazine. Second, we prepared press releases on the survey and sent them to all newspapers and media outlets. Third, our Chairman, who is a minister of religion, wrote a letter to all churches in the target wards, which we sent out to all denominations of churches, giving information about the survey and asking for co-operation.

From the sample, we also knew that we would probably survey disproportionate numbers of Catholics, since the wards with the highest death rates were disproportionately Catholic. We were also concerned that this would be compounded by a low response rate amongst Protestants. However, it emerged on analysis of the pilot and of the wards sampled, that the relatively high number of Catholics in the sample was a feature of the sampling procedures. Nonetheless, given the uncertain political climate at the time, together with the sensitive nature of the survey, we considered it necessary to disseminate as much information as possible, in order to help maximise our response rate. A deterioration in the political situation around Christmas 1997 slowed the fieldwork down, and meant an unforseeably long period in the field - from mid October 1997 until early March 1998. However, the fieldwork eventually concluded and a clean SPSS[3] file was delivered at the end of April 1998.

Sampling

The initial proposal specified 3,000 attempted questionnaires or roughly one in 500 of the region's population. The challenge was to find a sampling procedure that would adequately reflect the population as a whole while simultaneously generating sufficient cases in those areas most affected by the Troubles to make their analysis worthwhile. In order to do so the following sample procedure was adopted:

From the database of Troubles-related deaths, a calculation was made of the number of residents of each Northern Ireland ward who had died in the Troubles. This was achieved by translating postal codes into ward locations. The procedure ignored the deaths of non-Northern Ireland residents to concentrate exclusively on the regional population. A figure for ward population was constructed by taking the average from each of the 1971, '81 and '91 Censuses in recognition that the deaths occurred over a 30 year period. From these two figures a ward 'death rate' was then constructed and wards were ranked in descending order. Three groups of wards were identified:

* Those with the highest death rates (7 or more deaths per 1,000 population) - ten wards;
* Those with medium death rates (ranging from 2 to 6.9 deaths per 1,000) - 122 wards;
* And, those with low death rates (ranging from 0 to 1.9 deaths per 1,000) - 424 wards.

From each group, 10 wards were selected on a random basis. The sampling fractions were thus 1, .082 and .024. Sampling was thus proportionate to the intensity of politically motivated deaths. The end result was a sample of 30 wards stratified by death rates. Within each group of wards, 1,000 cases were selected. The number of cases in individual wards was proportionate to the ward's share of its group population and these were also selected randomly from the 1997 electoral register.

Administering the Questionnaire

In total, 57 people of the 3,000 written to contacted our office. Of these, seven wanted to make specific arrangements to meet the interviewer, as they weren't always available. Eighteen wrote letters, mostly saying politely that they did not want to participate; three people wrote saying that they were disabled or infirm and felt it "inappropriate" to participate. One person wrote, putting forward the view that the Troubles were caused by "our departure from the Lord and the Word" and that that was all she wanted to say on the subject. Another wrote, saying that "the following testimony is the only contact I intend to have with the study team per se, and went on, "As with the majority of such studies as yours, your remit begins in the middle and asks all the wrong questions." This correspondent finished, "The theme of the 'troubles' is a string of death, injury, and tears. The "cost of the 'troubles'" is the cost of Eden's apple bite:- knowledge, sorrow, and a taste of freedom!" One letter said simply, "I do not wish to participate in your survey. The troubles has not affected me greatly over the years, as it has done to others. Therefore it would be of more beneficial (sic) to your work if you found someone to else to help you. I do not wish to be contacted further, and I thank you for writing to me in the first place."

The interviewers began work, and reported to debriefing sessions any particular difficulties they were encountering. In more middle class area, or areas least affected by the Troubles interviewers reported lower response rates. Some interviewees reported reluctance on the part of respondents to participate in a survey related to delicate political issues. It is also possible that some of those who refused to participate did so because they did not wish to reveal painful experiences of the Troubles to a stranger.

An interim report on fieldwork written in December 1997 shows fourteen wards with below ten completed questionnaires. At this stage in the fieldwork management it was necessary to analyse the reasons for low returns in some wards, and rectify any problems. Two hypotheses were formed about the difficulties. Either the difficulties were caused by local conditions and resistance in certain wards, or the problem was the performance of the interviewer in that ward. Reallocations of interviewers who had achieved high return rates in their own wards, to wards

---

[3] SPSS is an acronym for Statistical Package for the Social Sciences, a statistical software package commonly used to undertake statistical analysis of data sets generated by surveys.

with low return rates demonstrated that much of the problem was due to interviewers, and our "super-interviewers" were able to increase the returns in most of the wards where we had concerns. However, two wards, Newtownhamilton and Ballymacarrett, proved to be impossible for even our "super-interviewers" to obtain returns from, both returning less than ten questionnaires. In the case of Newtownhamilton, we subsequently learned that there was a great deal of strong feeling in the area about the effects of the Troubles, witnessed by the formation of a local pressure group in mid 1998. In the case of Ballymacarrett, the cause of the low return rate is unknown.

The following table identifies the 30 wards, indicates the attempted number of interviews and the number of questionnaires actually completed.

Table 1.1: Numbers and rates of response by ward						
Ward Name	Attempted	Ineligibles	Attempted less ineligibles	Achieved	Completion Rate	Ward Pop 91	Achieved as % of Ward Pop
Wards with high death rates							
Falls	111	19	92	58	63.0%	521	1.1%
Ardoyne	119	15	104	74	71.2%	6340	1.2%
Clonard	106	32	74	41	55.4%	5475	0.7%
Waterworks	119	5	114	70	61.4%	5742	1.2%
Whiterock	102	14	88	74	84.1%	5285	1.4%
New Lodge	118	8	110	50	45.5%	6385	0.8%
Valley	66	11	55	24	43.6%	2316	1.0%
Ballymacarret	100	3	97	6	6.2%	4899	0.1%
Upper Springfield	111	14	97	70	72.2%	6186	1.1%
Newtownhamilton	47	14	33	4	12.1%	2336	0.2%
High totals	999	135	864	471	54.5%	50179	0.9%
Wards with middle range death rates							
Charlemont	79	9	70	49	70%	2194	2.2%
Creggan South	80	19	61	45	73.8%	2361	1.9%
Killycolpy	69	4	66	50	75.6%	2199	2.3%
Carrigatuke	72	7	65	36	53.4%	2157	1.7%
Fortwilliam	169	22	147	56	38.1%	5114	1.1%
Ballysillan	194	26	168	36	21.4%	4857	0.7%
Newtownbutler	83	4	79	62	78.5%	2285	2.7%
Termon	74	2	72	43	59.7%	2245	1.9%
Annagh	89	11	79	43	54.4%	2353	1.8%
Corcrain	90	21	69	55	79.7%	2961	1.9%
Middle totals	999	125	876	475	54.2%	28726	1.7%

Table 1.1: Numbers and rates of response by ward						
Ward Name	Attempted	Ineligibles	Attempted less ineligibles	Achieved	Completion Rate	Ward Pop 91	Achieved as % of Ward Pop
Wards with low death rates						
Ballee	80	14	66	27	40.9%	2485	1.1%
Coalisland South	82	3	79	58	73.4%	2023	2.9%
Drumgullion	104	11	93	42	45.2%	3025	1.4%
Fairy Water	69	12	57	31	54.4%	1872	1.7%
Finaghy	188	48	140	71	50.7%	6702	1.1%
Gilnahirk	97	1	96	21	21.9%	2920	0.7%
Glen	104	11	93	56	60.2%	3038	1.8%
Harmony Hill	113	2	111	24	21.6%	3839	0.6%
Lawrencetown	77	1	76	49	64.5%	1966	2.5%
Randalstown	86	10	76	31	40.8%	2061	1.5%
Low totals	1000	113	887	410	46.2%	29931	1.4%
Overall Totals & percentages	2998	373	2627	1356	51.6%	108836	1.2%

The first issue that struck us was the high level of ineligibles (12.4%) drawn in the sample, although the rate was 25.5% in one ward (Finaghy). We used the 1997 electoral list, which has subsequently been the subject of scrutiny as a result of doubts about its validity, and this is reflected in our sample. This immediately reduced the size of our valid sample. Within wards, there was significant variation in the numbers of achieved interviews and therefore of completion rates. The very low response rates recorded in two wards, Ballymacarrett and Newtownhamilton, are apparent in Table 1.1, and this was in spite of deploying new interviewers in these wards to eliminate the possibility that the low rate was due to interviewer performance. This also translates in variation in coverage of ward populations which in the case of five wards: Clonard, Ballymacarett, Newtownhamilton, Ballysillan and Harmony Hill, fall below 1% of the ward population. Our overall coverage of the wards with high death rates (0.9%) was lower than for medium death rate (1.7%) or low death rate (1.4%) wards. However, it should be noted that each questionnaire elicits data on a household, so that in all, some data was collected on over 4,500 individuals. In some wards, completed questionnaires represented over two per cent of the ward population. In others, however, the figure was closer to 0.2 per cent. Nevertheless, certain questionnaire data relate to a higher proportion of the ward population - around 4.0%.

Arguably, the sampling procedure, which aims to collect the largest amount of data in the wards which have been most affected, complicate the survey's ability to be representative of the Northern Ireland population. However, there is no perfect sampling procedure particularly for a survey in which the aim was to be able to compare those areas where the experience of violence was greatest with those which had no direct experience of it. When we come to analyse the data, we have analysed the data from the three locations separately for this reason.

The end result of our efforts was 1356 completed questionnaires probing some of the worst experiences of people's lives, with just over a third from those areas where the Troubles were most intense. The selected wards represent about six per cent of the region's population.

Section 2

Basic Description of the Sample

The chosen sampling procedure selected three separate groups of wards in order to compare different levels of experience of the Troubles. Since it is likely that those interviewed in each of these areas have different characteristics in addition to exposure to violence, this description has a separate section for each group.

High Intensity Wards

In all, 471 people were interviewed within the high intensity wards. 53.7 per cent were women and 46.3 per cent men. The group was distributed across the following age bands:

Table 2.1 Age Distribution in High Intensity Wards								
Age Percentage:	15-19	20-24	25-39	40-59	60-64	65-79	80+	Total
	.55	12.1	35.7	28.8	7.3	8.9	1.6	437

Almost two thirds of respondents were aged between 25 and 59. Only just over one in 20 was aged 19 or less. Compared to the Northern Ireland population estimate for 1995, there were higher percentages of respondents in the 20-24 band (12.1% compared to 7.6%) and the 25-39 band (28.2% compared to 22.8%)

Two fifths of respondents were married and a further third was single. 11.2 per cent were separated or divorced, 8.4 per cent were widowed and 5.4 per cent were single parents. Just over 40 per cent lived in one or two person households, another third lived in three or four person households. Just 4.5 per cent lived in households with seven or more members.

62 per cent had no qualifications compared to only four per cent with an undergraduate or professional qualification. 70 per cent claimed that they had not been in paid employment in the previous seven days. However, 35 per cent reported that they were in full-time work, a further 10 per cent in part-time work and a further four per cent in training. Half of the respondents reported that they were either unemployed or permanently sick.

Almost three-quarters of respondents were living in rented accommodation with less than a quarter home owners.

94 per cent of those interviewed in this ward group were catholic with just five per cent Protestant.

Middle Intensity Wards

474 respondents came from middle intensity wards. Of these 48.9 per cent were male and 51.1 per cent female. Their age range in described in Table 2.2.

Table 2.2 Age Distribution in Middle Intensity Wards							
Age Bnd Percentage: 15-19	20-24	25-39	40-59	60-64	65-79	80+	Total
4.3	9.9	31.1	34.1	7.6	10.4	2.6	463

In one respect, the age structure is similar as in high intensity wards. 65.2 per cent of respondents were aged between 25 and 59. However, there was a higher percentage of older people (13% aged 65 or more) and a lower percentage of young people (14.2% less than 25). Household structure was similar to high intensity wards – 41 per cent in one or two person households and a further 30 per cent in three or four person households.

More than half of the respondents (54%) were married and a further 34% were single. A total of just over 10 per cent were either widowed, single parents or separated/divorced. This is in marked contrast to the high intensity wards.

46.6% had no qualifications and over a third of respondents had either O'/A' levels, degrees or professional qualifications. 50 per cent had been in employment in the previous week. Three-quarters were either in full-time or part-time work while a quarter reported that they were either unemployed or permanently sick.

Almost 70 per cent were home owners and less than 30 per cent claimed that they were living in rented accommodation

62 per cent of respondents in these wards were Catholic and 37 per cent were Protestant

Low Intensity Wards

Low intensity wards contributed the smallest number to the overall sample (410), but the highest proportion of women – 56 per cent compared to 44 per cent men.

Least Intensity	15-19	20-24	25-39	40-59	60-64	65-79	80+	Total
Table 2.3 Age Distribution in Low Intensity Wards								
	.4.4	9.9	26.9	33.8	8.6	12.6	3.7	405

The majority of the population was again aged between 25 and 59 (60.7%). However, the percentage over 65 was just over 16 per cent indicating a relative larger proportion of elderly people than in either of the other two ward groups.

These wards also had the highest proportion of respondents married (61.3) and the lowest percentage of single people (21.3%). Just less than nine per cent of respondents were widowed and 8.4 per cent separated or divorced. Less than half of one per cent of respondents were single parents.

The percentage of respondents with no qualifications was similar to middle intensity wards (45.5%) but a further 43 per cent had O'/A' levels, degrees or professional qualifications.

54 per cent had been in employment in the previous week and 86 per cent claimed to be in fill-time or part-time work. Only 16 per cent claimed that they were unemployed or permanently sick.

72 per cent of respondents identified themselves as homeowners while 28 per cent were renting.

Just over 50 per cent of the respondents in these wards were Protestant and 47 per cent Catholic.

Different Territories?

The 30 wards were selected simply on the criterion of death rates. Yet substantial other differences also emerge. The contrast is most obvious between high intensity and low intensity wards. The former is predominantly Catholic, low skilled, high unemployment with low percentages having qualifications and a significant number of lone parents. The latter has a majority of Protestants, with almost half with qualifications, high rates of employment and lone parents almost non-existent.

The main purpose of the next section is to explore how these different territories experienced the Troubles.

Section 3
Analysis of Results

Individual and Area Characteristics - Experiencing the Troubles

Previous analysis of violence in Northern Ireland undertaken by the Costs of the Troubles highlighted the significance of certain key variables - location, gender, religion, age, and socio-economic status. It has been demonstrated that these are crucially associated with an individual's experience of the Troubles. In addition, the majority of direct causalities of violence have been male, suggesting that the Troubles have been a predominantly male phenomenon. This section of the report explores each of these variables. The predominant form of analysis is crosstabulation given the categorical nature of the variables concerned. For each of the crosstabulations, Chi Square tests were performed to ensure that the differences recorded were systematic rather than random. The intention was to use a significance level of .05. However, given the large number of crosstabulations, this was increased to .005. This is a more rigorous significance level than normally applied. However, with the .05 level, any one of 20 crosstabulations may have random rather than systematic differences. In this exercise over 80 crosstabulations were performed increasing the number of dubious relationships within the set. Raising the level to .005 may exclude certain relationships that were significant but this was regarded as more acceptable. All reported differences are significant at this level unless otherwise indicated.

Location

In the analysis of the deaths' database we commented on its uneven spatial distribution of political violence in Northern Ireland. Certain areas have suffered disproportionately. This patterning of the conflict was the primary reason for the choice of sample procedure used. In order to analyse the role of location in the Troubles, a new variable was created with just three values: wards with the highest intensity of violence; wards with medium intensity of violence and wards with low intensity.

Ideally, analysis by individual ward would have reveal further detail in the distribution of Troubles' effects. However, since some wards have very low returns, the analysis only works at the level of ward group.

It should be said at the onset that these groups of wards were distinguished by more than just their level of violence. Table 3.1 records reported weekly household income for each of the three groups of wards.

£ per Week	Table 3.1 Percentages of Households in Various Income categories		
	Highest Intensity	Middle Intensity	Least Intensity
<£100	24.5	12.6	5.3
£100-249	45.6	38.2	18.5
£250-499	15.0	13.5	12.8
£500-999	4.8	4.3	3.7
N =	147	207	243

This table does not report missing values, therefore totals will not equal 100%

The group with the highest intensity of violence was characterised by households with extremely low incomes. Almost a quarter reported household income of less than £100 per week. 70 per cent had incomes less than £250 per week. Indeed for the lower income categories, household income varies inversely with degree of violence. Thus, the wards with least violence had the lowest proportion of households in the bottom income categories. While not shown on the table, they also had the highest proportion in the upper income categories.

Elsewhere (Fay, Morrissey and Smyth, 1998) we argue that there was not a high correlation between spatial indices of deprivation and ward death rates throughout Northern Ireland. It was hypothesised that the relationship was obscured by the inclusion of deaths of members of the security forces who did not tend to live in areas of acute deprivation. Here, however, the selection of the group of wards with highest death rates for local residents also involved selecting some of the region's most deprived wards.

Table 3.2 offers a profile of households and respondents in each of these ward groups.

Table 3.2 Socio-economic Profile of households in each ward group			
	Highest Intensity	Middle Intensity	Least Intensity
No Household Members receiving benefits	16.2%	46.7%	51.7%
No Household Member in Employment	57.0%	29.2%	29.8%
Respondents with no qualifications	62.1%	46.6%	45.5%
Residing in Public or Previously Public Sector Housing	86.1%	32.7%	32.6%
Residing in Rented Housing	74.7%	30.6%	28.0%
Living in a Religiously Segregated Area	91.9%	50.1%	29.9%
Number	471	474	407

Again, the wards with the highest intensity of violence stand out. These are characterised by low levels of employment, high benefits dependency and respondents with no educational qualifications concentrated in public sector, rented accommodation, for the most part religiously segregated.

The labour market profile of respondents in these wards presents a similar picture.

Table 3.3 Labour market profile of respondents in each ward group			
	Highest Intensity	Middle Intensity	Least Intensity
full-time work	99	193	170
%	35.5	58.0	66.9
part-time work	28	51	42
%	10.0	15.3	16.5
In training	10	2	1
%	3.6	0.6	0.4
Unemployed	109	44	22
%	39.11	3.2	8.7
Permanently sick or disabled	33	43	19
%	11.8	12.9	7.5
Total	279	333	254
%	100	100	100

In the wards that experienced the greatest degree of violence, lower percentages of respondents were in work while the percentage unemployed was three times that in middle intensity wards and more than four times that in low intensity wards.

While this is to be expected, it also complicates the analysis. Looking for specifically Troubles' related effects requires separating out other factors like deprivation. In practice, this is rarely easy to accomplish. Of course, it has been argued that deprivation and violence are intimately related - that grievance at inequality and discrimination fuels violence. However, such arguments could be equally applied to peripheral housing estates in Britain where poverty and squalor can be linked to local crime. Some of the difficulties in identifying the impact of the Troubles will emerge in this analysis.

Table 3.4 Percentages Reporting Experience of the Troubles by Location			
Experience of the Troubles	Highest Intensity	Middle Intensity	Least Intensity
A lot	25.9	11.9	5.5
Quite a lot	28.9	16.6	12.0
Some	24.2	29.6	26.3
A little	10.2	17.9	16.8
Very Little	9.9	20.3	35.3
None	0.9	3.6	4.3
N=	463	469	400

Given how these wards were sampled, it is unsurprising that the 'highest intensity' wards should record such scores. Nevertheless, almost 55 per cent of respondents reported a lot or quite a lot experience of the Troubles. A further quarter reported some experience of the Troubles. Such findings suggest that for almost 30 years in certain places in Northern Ireland, the Troubles have been nearly a way of life.

Interestingly, when respondents were asked to specify the nature of their experience, a smaller proportion in the highest intensity wards referred to news reports. This might suggest that the Troubles were more a lived reality than a series of media events. The kinds of experience reported more frequently in these wards were 'being stopped and searched by the security forces', 'being wary in the presence of people from the other community', 'having to take extra security precautions to secure my home or workplace 'having to change normal routes, routines or habits because of safety'. With other questions, for example, 'being stopped at a checkpoint', the frequency of the experience was no higher than for the other two groups of wards. For the group of health questions in the questionnaire, those in wards with the most intense violence, consistently reported more health problems than in other wards. Although this may reflect health problems associated with deprivation, a third of respondents indicated that troubles related incidents had an effect on their general health and a fifth reported similarly for troubles related bereavement. There is thus some evidence that the troubles have impacted negatively on health, particularly in wards with the highest levels of violence.

For other types of experience of the Troubles, the highest intensity wards stood out. The following tables relate to direct experience of the Troubles

Table 3.5: The experience of having to conceal things in order to feel safe			
	Highest Intensity	Middle Intensity	Least Intensity
very often	71	30	14
%	15.2	6.4	3.4
occasionally	188	59	35
%	40.2	12.6	8.6
seldom	90	75	75
%	19.2	16.0	18.4
never	119	305	283
%	25.4	65.0	69.5
Total	468	469	407
%	100	100	100

Note: Totals in each response category in this table do not always match those in Table 3.24 because of differential missing values.

The high intensity wards reported in the 'very often' category more than twice as much as in middle intensity wards and more than four times as often as those from low intensity wards. A similar picture emerges for the experience of 'having to listen to my tradition being criticised or abused'.

Table 3.6: Experience of having to listen to my tradition being criticised or abused			
	Highest Intensity	Middle Intensity	Least Intensity
very often	172	62	30
%	36.8	13.2	7.4
occasionally	192	125	74
%	41.1	26.6	18.2
seldom	48	93	123
%	10.3	19.8	30.3
never	55	190	179
%	11.8	40.4	44.1
Total	467	470	406
%	100	100	100

This pattern is repeated across almost all the variables for direct experience of the Troubles. Indeed, feeling very often blamed for the Troubles scored ten times higher in highest intensity, compared to least intensity wards. In the highest intensity wards, 28 per cent reported having their home attacked very often or occasionally - 10 per cent reported that they had had their home destroyed!

Table 3.7 Experience of being Caught Up in a Riot by Location			
	Highest Intensity	Middle Intensity	Least Intensity
several times	180	58	9
%	38.5	12.4	2.2
more than once	129	44	38
%	27.6	9.4	9.4
once	47	38	42
%	10.0	8.1	10.3
never	112	329	317
%	23.9	70.1	78.1
Total	468	469	406
%	100	100	100

In the high intensity wards, almost 40 per cent of respondents reported being caught up in riots several times, almost three-quarters had been in a riot at least once.

Table 3.8 Experience of having a Neighbour Killed by Location		
	Highest Intensity	Middle Intensity	Least Intensity
several times	31	13	4
%	6.6	2.8	1.0
more than once	76	48	51
%	16.2	10.3	12.5
once	134	69	29
%	28.6	14.7	7.1
never	227	338	323
%	48.5	72.2	79.4
Total	468	468	407
%	100	100	100

Over half of respondents in high intensity wards reported having a neighbour killed, compared to one in five in the least intensity wards. Just less than half reported having a friend killed. More than a third reported having a member of the immediate family injured. A fifth had a member of their immediate family killed.

In terms of attributing the responsibility for the Troubles, those in wards least affected by the Troubles tended to blame Republican and Loyalist paramilitary organisations with combined scores between 75 and 80 per cent for 'responsible' or 'most responsible'. Wards with highest intensity tended to blame Loyalist, though not Republican, paramilitaries. Most of all, however, they tended to blame, the RUC, the British Army, Loyalist politicians and British politicians with scores in excess of 75 per cent for each. This result is also affected by the religious composition of these wards, which tend to be predominantly Catholic.

Moreover, individuals living in these high intensity wards felt more strongly that their lives had been altered by the Troubles.

Table 3.9: The Extent to which Experience of the Troubles Affected Individual lives		
	Highest Intensity	Middle Intensity	Least Intensity
complete change	81	12	6
%	17.4	2.6	1.5
radical change	51	42	26
%	10.9	9.0	6.5
some change	198	199	124
%	42.5	42.4	31.0
small impact	113	171	190
%	24.2	36.5	47.5
not at all	23	45	54
%	4.9	9.6	13.5
Total	466	469	400
%	100	100	100

Just over 28 per cent reported either a 'radical change' or a 'complete change' compared to 11.6 per cent in wards of next intensity. The proportion reporting some form of change was almost twice as high as in the least intensity wards.

Severe Experience of the Troubles and Effects by location

The relationship between the most severe experience of the Troubles and most severe impact appears to be significant. Appendix 4 shows in Tables 3.39- 3.41 the breakdown of severity of experience in high, medium and low intensity locations.

Table 3.39 shows that 39 respondents in high intensity areas reported both 'a lot' of experience of the Troubles and that the Troubles have made 'a complete change' in their lives. These account for 32.5% of respondents who report a lot of experience of the Troubles, and 48% of respondents who report that the Troubles have made a complete change in their lives. This compares to only 7 respondents in medium violence locations (Table 3.40) and 3 in low violence locations (Table 3.41).

Tables 3.39 - 3,41 show that whereas 32.5% of those in high violence areas report a lot of experience of the Troubles, only 12.5% report similarly in medium intensity areas, but 13.6%

report a lot of experience in low intensity areas. Between the three areas, however, the tendency was for those in high intensity areas to report higher levels of experience and more severe effects than in either of the other two areas.

Table 4.3 demonstrates how the responses in low intensity areas tend to fall in the less intense effects and less experience of the Troubles.

Table 3.42 in Appendix 4 examines the kind of help used by respondents in each of the three locations. In this breakdown of where respondents obtained help by location, significant differences between the different groups of wards emerge. Those in high intensity locations obtain help more frequently from all but two sources - the Samaritans and a faith healer. However, the numbers involved are so small that they do not affect the overall significant pattern - much larger numbers from high intensity areas seeking help.

There is variation between the three locations in the pattern of where help was most frequently obtained. Areas of highest intensity sought help from GP/local doctor, chemist, local politician, community worker, social security agency, other voluntary organisation and lawyer/solicitor in that order. Respondents in areas of medium violence also sought help from their GP/local doctor most frequently, but second most frequent was their lawyer/solicitor, followed by their minister/priest, chemist, local politician, psychiatrist, and counsellor. (The use of a psychiatrist may be explained in some instances by the need for psychiatric reports in cases where financial compensation is sought.) In areas of low violence, the pattern differs again. There, respondents sought help most frequently from their GP/local doctor, then from their minister or priest, then lawyer or solicitor, local politician, chemist, community worker, and community nurse.

It would seem that a higher percentage of those in areas of high intensity violence seek and obtain help of any kind, and when they obtain help, they are less likely to use their minister/priest, solicitor, psychiatrist, counsellor or community nurse than those in medium or low intensity areas. Conversely they were more likely than any of the other locations to use the social security agency and other voluntary organisations. The higher levels of deprivation in these areas may explain this.

Significant differences also emerged between the three areas in terms of where respondents received their best help. Table 3.43 in Appendix 4 shows the results by location.

Table 3.43 in Appendix 4 shows that in all three locations, respondents reported receiving their best help from their spouse, followed by either parents or other close family. This was followed by close friends, neighbours, local doctor or children. Local doctors were the most likely non-family source of help to be regarded as a source of good help. However, the overall results show that overwhelmingly family, friends and neighbours have provided the most valued help with the effects of the Troubles.

Table 3.10 describes how respondents evaluated the help they had received. It does not reflect responses from the substantial number of respondents to whom this question did not apply, since they did not seek help.

Table 3.10: Do you think the help you received was satisfactory?							
Was help satisfactory?	Count (% within location)	Highest Intensity		Middle Intensity		Least Intensity	
		Yes	No	Yes	No	Yes	No
Sympathetic	Count	191	30	66	16	41	11
& helpful	%	45.4	7.1	14.4	3.5	10.6	2.8
Adequate	Count	36	57	25	44	17	32
only	%	8.8	14.0	5.5	9.7	4.4	8.3
Insensitive	Count	8	80	5	63	1	49
	%	2.0	19.9	1.1	13.8	.3	11.9
Harmful	Count	5	83	1	67	1	46
	%	1.2	20.6	.2	14.7	.3	11.9
Judgemental	Count	8	81	7	61	3	11.4
	%	2.0	20.1	1.5	13.4	.8	2.8
Critical	Count	6	82	5	62	3	44
of me	%	1.5	20.4	1.1	13.7	8	11.4
Couldn't	Count	6	79	2	59	5	39
find help	%	1.5	19.6	.4	13	1.3	10.1
Didn't need	Count	54	77	70	63	103	38
help	%	13.0	18.6	15.4	13.8	26.4	9.7

In all cases, with the exception of the last category, 'Did not need help', response levels are highest in the high intensity location, reflecting the greater use of help. Generally, help was evaluated positively, with a small but consistent minority of respondents in all three locations reporting unsatisfactory experience of help received.

Table 3.11 reports on difficulties in finding help.

Table 3.11	Difficulty in finding help			
		Highest Intensity	Middle Intensity	Least Intensity	Total
Didn't know	Count	24	38	11	73
where to look	%	32.88	52.05	15.07	100.00
	% within Location	9.38	31.93	8.73	14.57
Unable to find satisfactory help to meet needs	Count	10	7	7	24
	%	41.67	29.17	29.17	100.00
	% within Location	3.91	5.88	5.56	4.79
Not able to look	Count	7	4	0	11
	%	63.64	36.36		100.00
	% within Location	2.73	3.36		2.20
Didn't believe anything could help at the time	Count	151	8	22	181
	%	83.43	4.42	12.15	100.00
	% within Location	58.98	6.72	17.46	36.13
Other	Count	64	62	86	212
	%	30.19	29.25	40.57	100.00
	% within Location	25.00	52.10	68.25	42.32
Total	Count	256	119	126	501
	%	51.10	23.75	25.15	100.00

Again, results show consistently higher responses in the high intensity location, perhaps related to the greater use of help in those locations. However, a higher number of respondents in the medium intensity areas indicated that they did not know where to look for help. This suggests that those in high intensity locations may be more knowledgeable about available help, perhaps related to their greater level of expressed need and reported usage of existing sources of help.

Table 3.12 examines the use of medication for symptoms related to the Troubles.

Table 3.12 Have you ever taken medication from any source?					
		Highest Intensity	Middle Intensity	Least Intensity	Total
yes	Count	109	54	35	198
	% within response	55.05	27.27	17.68	100
	% within Location	23.75	11.95	9.02	15.24
no	Count	350	398	353	1101
	% within response	31.79	36.15	32.06	100
	% within Location	76.25	88.05	90.98	84.76
Total	Count	459	452	388	1299
	%	35.33	34.80	29.87	100
	% within Location	100	100	100	100

Table 3.12 shows clearly a significantly higher level of medication usage among respondents in the high intensity areas. Medium intensity areas come second and low intensity areas have the lowest reported usage of medication.

Table 3.13 examines the duration of medication use.

Table 3.13: Duration of consumption of medication		Highest Intensity	Middle Intensity	Least Intensity	Total
Occasionally/ single dose	Count	17	8	8	33
	% within response	51.52	24.24	24.24	100.00
	% within Location	15.32	14.55	21.62	16.26
One/Several days	Count	4	9	1	14
	% within response	28.57	64.29	7.14	100.00
	% within Location	3.60	16.36	2.70	6.90
Two weeks or less	Count	3	6	1	10
	% within response	30	60	10	100
	% within Location	2.70	10.91	2.70	4.93
Two weeks to	Count	3	5	1	9
	% within response	33.33	55.56	11.11	100.00
	% within Location	2.70	9.09	2.70	4.43
1 month - 1 year	Count	12	9	6	27
	% within response	44.44	33.33	22.22	100.00
	% within Location	10.81	16.36	16.22	13.30
1 - 5 years	Count	7	9	4	20
	% within response	35	45	20	100
	% within Location	6.31	16.36	10.81	9.85
More than 5 years	Count	7	4	3	14
	% within response	50.00	28.57	21.43	100.00
	% within Location	6.31	7.27	8.11	6.90
Permanently	Count	58	5	13	76
	% within response	76.32	6.58	17.11	100.00
	% within Location	52.25	9.09	35.14	37.44
Total	Count	111	55	37	203
	% within response	54.68	27.09	18.23	100.00
	% within Location	100	100	100	100

There were marked differences between the three locations in terms of use of medication. Perhaps the most startling figure to emerge form this analysis is the 52.3% of respondents using medication in high intensity locations who are on medication permanently. The equivalent percentage for low intensity areas (35.1%) is higher than that for medium intensity areas (9.1%). Short term consumption (one day to one month is highest in medium intensity areas, as is consumption for periods of 1-5 years. Long term consumption (5 years to permanently) and occasional use is by far the highest in high intensity locations.

Finally, respondents were asked to account for the medication given to them as a result of the effects of the Troubles, in terms of the purpose for which it was prescribed.

Table 3.14 Purpose for which Troubles-related medication was prescribed

Purpose of medication		Highest Intensity Yes	Middle Intensity Yes	Least Intensity Yes	Total
Help you sleep single dose	Count	83	33	26	224
	% within location	75.5	44.0	66.7	
Calm you down	Count	90	41	19	222
	% within location	81.8	56.9	47.5	
Give you a lift in in mood	Count	60	25	7	210
	% within location	60.0	34.2	18.9	
To even out your moods	Count	55	18	1	205
	% within location	56.1		25.4	2.8
Kill pain	Count 204	58		13	8
	% within location	59.8		18.3	22.2
Keep away memories	Count 180	22		14	11
	% within location	30.6		19.7	29.7
Treat a physical condition	Count 181	37		6	12
	% within location	50.7	8.5	32.4	
Other	Count	8	1	3	148
	% within location	15.4	1.6	9.4	

Again, significant differences emerge between the three locations, with respondents in the high intensity locations out-numbering those in both of the other two locations in positive responses to all of the questions. Respondents, using drugs in high intensity locations, were most likely to be using them for sleep disturbance, sedation or anti-depressive purposes, as were residents in medium intensity locations, whereas respondents in low intensity locations were most likely to be using them for sleep disturbance, sedation and pain control. However, the overall level of drug use for all purposes (with the exception of the "other" category) was again higher in high intensity locations.

Indeed, when it came to reporting particular effects, the following is illustrative of the sharp differences amongst these groups of wards:

- Over a third of respondents in wards of highest intensity reported painful memories compared to a fifth in the middle intensity group:

- Over a quarter in wards of highest intensity reported dreams and nightmares compared to an eighth in the middle intensity group;

- A third in wards of highest intensity reported involuntary recall compared to an eighth in the middle intensity group;

- 30 per cent in wards of highest intensity felt some form of guilt at surviving compared to 11 per cent in the middle intensity group;

- 22 per cent in wards of highest intensity reported an increase in alcohol consumption related to the Troubles compared to just over four per cent in middle intensity wards;

- those in high intensity wards had more severe experiences and reported more severe effects of the Troubles than those in the other two wards;

- Those in high intensity wards sought help more frequently than those in other wards;

- In all cases, help was sought primarily from friends and immediate family although some differences emerged in help sought outside the family between the three locations;

- Over 40 per cent of those who sought help in high intensity wards were unable to find satisfactory help, compared to 29 per cent in medium intensity and 29 per cent in low intensity wards;

- Over 83 per cent in high intensity wards believed that nothing could help them, compared to just over 4 per cent in medium intensity and just over 12 per cent in low intensity wards;

- over 23 per cent had taken medication in high intensity wards compared to almost 12 per cent in medium wards and just over 9 per cent in low intensity wards;

- of those who used medication, over 52 per cent of those in high intensity wards were on medication permanently, compared to 9 per cent in medium intensity and 35 per cent for low intensity wards;

- those using medication in high intensity wards were likely to be using it for sleep disturbance, sedation or anti-depressive purposes, whereas those in low intensity wards used them for pain control rather than for anti-depressive purposes.

Indeed for every 'effects' variable, marked differences are observable. Differential experience and effects of the Troubles would seem to be conditioned more by location than either gender or religion. These responses suggest that there have been three key dimensions to life in the areas most affected by the Troubles:

- first, there is the much greater exposure to Troubles-related events both from paramilitary organisations and the security forces - a set of experiences almost unmatched in the rest of Northern Ireland (this group of wards regularly reported experience of Troubles' related activity at twice the rate for middle wards and four times the rate for least intensity wards);

- second, there are insecurities and fears in being outside one's own area and an acute wariness of outsiders, for example reflected in efforts to conceal where one lives;

- third, there is a strong pattern of segregation - over a quarter of those from highest intensity wards who were employed, worked only with members of their own community, as we will discuss below.

As mentioned previously, these findings might seem to be an artefact of the sampling procedure. However, they are exactly what the sampling procedure was designed to illustrate, the stark and pervasive differences in people's lives resulting from continued proximity to violence.

Segregation

A further dimension of the issue of location is that of segregation. Previous research in a linked project, and a considerable volume of literature, point to the degree of religious segregation within the Northern Ireland community. This has been exacerbated by the Troubles where individuals and families fled from mixed areas to concentrate in places where they felt safe. However, those living in 'enclaves' have not been insulated from the Troubles. The following tables report on the responses of those living in segregated areas compared to non-segregated areas. One caution about attributing significance to these findings is that religious segregation is a widespread phenomenon. Nevertheless, over 500 respondents claimed that they did not live in such areas.

Table 3.15: Experience of the Troubles by Living in a Segregated Area		
Living in a Segregated Area		
	yes	no
A lot	166	30
%	21.4	5.5
Quite a lot	197	62
%	25.4	11.4
Some	205	147
%	26.4	27.0
A little	98	99
%	12.6	18.2
Very Little	100	178
%	12.9	32.7
None	10	28
%	1.3	5.1
Total	776	544
%	100	100

The percentage of respondents living in segregated areas who reported experiencing the Troubles 'a lot' was almost four times higher than for those who did not live in segregated areas. For 'quite a lot' the percentage was more than twice as great. Conversely, reports of 'very little' or 'none' constituted almost 40 per cent of those living in non-segregated areas compared to under 15 per cent in segregated areas.

Table 3.16 Effect of the Troubles on People's Lives		
by Living in A Segregated Area		
Living in a Segregated Area		
	yes	no
complete change	93	6
%	11.9	1.1
radical change	78	40
%	10.0	7.4
some change	320	195
%	41.1	35.8
small impact	242	227
%	31.1	41.7
not at all	46	76
%	5.9	14.0
Total 779 544		
% 100 100		

Similar differences appear in comparing the impact of the Troubles on people's lives. Over a fifth of those living in segregated areas reported a 'complete' or 'radical' change compared to a twelfth in non-segregated areas. In the latter over a half reported either a 'small impact' or 'not at all' compared to over a third in segregated areas.

The very sharp differences amongst the three locations in terms of experiences and effects may be the central finding of this survey. The remainder of the analysis looks at differences by gender, religion and age. In each case, the analysis is supplemented by examining differences amongst these variables by each of the three locations

Gender
Respondents were asked to report on the frequency of their experience of the Troubles.

Table 3.17 Gender By Experience of the Troubles			
	Male	Female	Total
A lot	105	93	198
%	17.2%	13.1%	15.0%
Quite a lot	124	136	260
%	20.3%	19.2%	19.7%
Some	182	173	355
%	29.7%	24.4%	26.9%
A little	82	114	196
%	13.4%	16.1%	14.8%
Very Little	106	169	275
%	17.3%	23.8%	20.8%
None	13	25	38
%	2.1%	3.5%	2.9%
Total	612	710	1322
%	100.0%	100.0%	100.0%

Although the analysis of deaths suggested that males have been the primary victims, the survey data paints a different picture. Certainly, a higher proportion of men claimed to have experience of the Troubles, but with these findings the relative gender differences are much less stark. 37.5 per cent of men claimed to have experienced the Troubles 'a lot' or 'quite a lot' compared to 22.3 per cent of women. Correspondingly, just fewer than 20 per cent of men and just over a quarter of women claimed very little or no experience. Such gender differences were reported within all three locations even though women's experiences were substantially higher in the high intensity ward group. For example, in that ward group 29.6 per cent of men and 22.8 per cent of women claimed 'a lot' of experience of the Troubles compared to 8.2 per cent and 3.6 per cent in the least intensity group. It would appear that male/female differences were less pronounced in the high intensity wards although the number reporting 'a lot' in the least intensity wards was very small (22 in total), only five per cent of all respondents in this group of wards. Moreover, the Chi Square values for the crosstabulations were .044 and .015.

The term 'experience' is subject to wide interpretation. Does living in Northern Ireland and seeing nightly news bulletins constitute an experience of the Troubles? When questioned about the nature of that experience, certain differences in the male/female experience emerged. Here only the category 'very often' is analysed, since it suggests that the Troubles were intrusive in individual lifestyle. Very high proportions of both had 'very often' encountered the Troubles in news reports. When it came to areas of individual active involvement, such as being in a bomb scare, or straying into an area where the person felt unsafe, or being stopped and searched by the security forces or feeling that they had to change normal routines, men experienced these roughly 50% more than women. It should be noted that for every variable, a minority of the sample reported often or very often. However, more than a third of males had been stopped and searched by the security forces.

Table 3.18 Types of Experience of the Troubles		
	male	female
News Reports		
very often	510	564
%	82.3	78.7
Bomb Scare		
very often	56	47
%	9.0	6.7
Unsafe Area		
very often	77	45
%	12.5	6.3
Stopped/Searched		
very often	227	144
%	36.6	20.0
Stopped/Checkpoint		
very often	286	226
%	46.1	35.1
Unable to Say what Think		
very often	126	119
%	20.4	16.6
Being Wary		
very often	86	81
%	13.9	11.3
Extra security precautions at home		
very often	91	79
%	14.7	11.0
Change Normal routines		
very often	83	68
%	13.4	9.5

Once again across the three locations - high, medium and low intensity - similar gender differences appeared across that range of responses.

A further set of experiences was explored in question 39 (see Appendix 1). There seems to be a set of experiences that both genders have had in common - listening to their own tradition being abused - feeling blamed for the Troubles - ending relationships because of the Troubles - having schooling disrupted - experience of paramilitary punishments (though not directly). For some of these variables, the proportion of women claiming to have experienced them was often actually higher than for men. In other issues, where the tension or conflict is interactive - being called sectarian names and, most of all getting into physical fights, the process has been more a male experience.

Table 3.19 Other Experiences of the Troubles		
	male	female
Being called sectarian names		
very often	71	44
%	11.5	6.1
Concealing things for safety reasons		
very often	79	53
%	12.7	7.4
Having to listen to own tradition being abused		
very often	135	129
%	21.8	18.0
Feeling blamed for the Troubles		
very often	66	85
%	10.7	11.8
having to end relationships because of community divide		
very often	25	23
%	4.0	3.2
Turn down work because of danger		
very often	44	34
%	7.1	4.8
Getting in physical fights because of the Troubles		
very often	23	5
%	3.7	0.7
Avoiding certain areas		
very often	133	113
%	21.5	15.8
Having schooling disrupted		
very often	19	29
%	3.1	4.1
Being forced to do things against my will		
very often	23	17
%	3.7	2.4
Experience of paramilitaries acting as punishment agencies		
very often	9	9
%	1.5	1.3
Paying protection money		
very often	1	1
%	0.2	0.1
So afraid, thought of leaving Northern Ireland.		
very often	23	17
%	3.7	2.4

In terms of the most direct experiences of the Troubles, gender differences existed, although, frequently the percentage values were low. For example, 26.7 per cent of men reported witnessing a shooting compared to 18.8 per cent of women. Very similar percentages reported that a member of the immediate family had been injured or killed.

These responses suggest that, while the analysis of the deaths' database pointed to the predominance of men amongst those killed in the Troubles, women have also seriously experienced a wide range of other aspects of the Troubles. The exact nature of that experience has tended to be different from men but women have also been substantially affected. Women in highest intensity wards have had greater experiences of the Troubles than women in other wards, but their experiences still remain less than men's experience in those wards. Nevertheless, women were very much part of the picture. Certainly, that women's experience of the Troubles is substantial is implied by the fact that women make up about nine per cent of all Troubles-related deaths.

Table 3.20 Effect on People's Lives by Gender		
	male	female
complete change	45	54
%	7.3	7.6
radical change	69	50
%	11.2	7.1
some change	241	278
%	39.1	39.2
small impact	195	272
%	31.7	38.4
not at all	66	55
%	10.7	7.8

As can be seen in Table 3.20, differences between respondents on the degree to which the Troubles affected their lives differ only marginally by gender. Indeed in highest intensity wards 18.2 per cent of women reported a complete change in their lives compared to 16.4 per cent of men. Thus, it would appear that although women in the sample generally, and in all three locations, report less experience of the Troubles, the impact on their lives has been equally severe

Religion

Predominantly, the analysis of the Troubles indicates that in both absolute and relative terms, Catholics have been more affected by violence. They make up the majority of all fatalities and the death rates for the region's Catholic population have been consistently higher than for the Protestant population. This has implications for the survey. The wards sampled because of their high death rates had a majority of Catholics and this influenced the responses. Analysis of the experience of the Troubles by religion thus has to make allowance for the higher number of Catholics in the sample.

Table 3.21	Experience of the Troubles by Religion		
	Catholic	Protestant	Other	Total
A lot	169	20	5	194
%	18.9	5.2	22.7	14.9
Quite a lot	204	53	3	260
%	22.8	13.8	13.6	20.0
Some	254	90	4	348
%	28.4	23.5	18.2	26.8
A little	113	71	3	187
%	12.6	18.5	13.6	14.4
Very Little	134	135	5	274
%	15.0	35.2	22.7	21.1
None	20	14	2	36
%	2.2	3.7	9.1	2.8
Total	894	383	22	1299
%	100	100	100	100

Although the respondent population consisted of two thirds Catholic and one third Protestant, the table above indicates that there is a relationship between religion and the experience of the Troubles. The percentage of Catholics reporting a lot of experience of the Troubles was more than three times higher than for Protestants. It can be seen that 18.9% and 22.8% of Catholics had a lot and quite a lot of experience, respectively. This can be compared to that of Protestants with 5.2% and 13.8%. It is also significant to note that 38.9% of Protestant have very little experience of the Troubles compared to 15% of Catholics for the same category. The majority of Catholics have some experience of the Troubles.

Despite the relatively large number of Catholics within the sample, the percentages claiming experience of the Troubles were higher still, suggesting, in line with the literature, that Catholic experience of conflict has been disproportionate. Even in the high intensity wards, this difference was sustained. There over a quarter of Catholics reported 'a lot' of experience of the Troubles with the comparable figure for Protestants remaining at five per cent. In fact, only 21 respondents in these wards were recorded as Protestant. Protestants made up 37 per cent of middle intensity wards and 51 per cent of low intensity wards. The religious composition of each group points to the general finding of greater Catholic experience of the Troubles.

This is reinforced by the findings of the next table, which compares the effect of the Troubles on people's lives, by religion.

Table 3.22 Religion by the Effect of the Troubles			
	Catholic	Protestant	Other	Total
complete change	90	8	1	99
%	10.1	2.1	4.5	7.6
radical change	96	14	2	112
%	10.7	3.6	9.1	8.6
some change	368	128	8	504
%	41.2	33.2	36.4	38.7
small impact	288	174	7	469
%	32.2	45.1	31.8	36.0
not at all	52	62	4	118
%	5.8	16.1	18.2	9.1
Total	894	386	22	1302
%	100	100	100	100

It is important to note that out of those experiencing a complete change 90.9% are Catholic compared to only 8.1% Protestant. Indeed, one in ten Catholic respondents reported that the Troubles had effected a complete change in their lives. In contrast, a majority of 52.5% of those in the 'Not at All' category are Protestant compared to 44.1% Catholic. In general, Catholics have experienced the more extreme effects of the Troubles with percentages skewed towards the upper end of the scale i.e. complete or radical change. In contrast, the effect of the Troubles has generally led to some change or a small impact upon Protestants. Once again similar differences between the two religions appeared even in high intensity wards.

The contrast between the opposite ends of the table - Catholics in the majority in the most affected categories, Protestants in the majority in the rest - reflects the general trend that the Catholics interviewed reported experiencing more the extreme effects of the Troubles compared to those reported by Protestants. 10.1% of Catholics and 2.1 % of Protestants in the 'Complete Change' category and 5.8% of Catholics and 16.1% of Protestants in the 'Not at All' category. It is also important to note that two thirds of the sample population are Catholic.

It is difficult to specify exactly what have been the differential impacts of the Troubles. On the assumption that the Troubles have had negative health impact, one comparison would be long-standing illness between the two religions.

	Table 3.23	Religion by Longstanding Illness		
	Catholic	Protestant	Other	Total
yes	189	112	5	306
%	20.9	28.6	22.7	23.2
no	715	279	17	1011
%	79.1	71.4	77.3	76.8
Total	904	391	22	1317
%	100	100	100	100

28.6 per cent of Protestants reported a long-standing illness compared to 20.9 per cent of Catholics. The proposition that Catholics because of their greater exposure to the Troubles might record greater concentrations of long-standing illness was not proved by this test.   Even in high intensity wards a higher percentage of Protestants reported long-standing illness. Nevertheless, other sharp and significant differences are observable between religions.

	Table 3.24	Painful Memories of the Troubles by Religion		
	Catholic	Protestant	Other	Total
frequently	82	22	1	105
	9.1	5.6	4.5	8.0
occasionally	173	36	2	211
	19.3	9.2	9.1	16.1
rarely	172	22	6	200
	19.2	5.6	27.3	15.3
never	431	305	13	749
	48.0	78.2	59.1	57.2
don't remember	40	5		45
	4.5	1.3		3.4
Total	898	390	22	1310

Catholics accounted for over 80 per cent of those suffering frequent and occasional painful memories of the Troubles. Just over 28 per cent of Catholics answered in these categories compared to just over 14 per cent of Protestants. Across a range of similar questions, including dreams of the Troubles, intrusive thoughts about Troubles related events, losing interest in normal activities and feelings of insecurity and jumpiness, showed similarly significant differences. Such feeling also embraced guilt at surviving. In this case, however, the differences between the two religions were more marginal, 7.7 per cent and 5.4 per cent respectively.

Table 3.25 Feelings of Shame and Guilt at Surviving the Troubles by religion

	Catholic	Protestant	Other	Total
frequently	23	9	0	32
%	2.6	2.3		2.5
occasionally	46	12	1	59
%	5.1	3.1	4.5	4.5
rarely	109	10	1	120
%	12.2	2.6	4.5	9.2
never	646	348	19	1013
%	72.1	89.7	86.4	77.6
don't remember	72	9	1	82
%	8.0	2.3	4.5	6.3
Total	896	388	22	1306
%	100	100	100	100

Respondents were asked if such effects had interfered with their lives. Almost 20 per cent of Catholics reported severe or moderate interference compared to nine per cent of Protestants, and these differences were consistent across the three locations.

In short, the evidence of greater Catholic experience of the Troubles is supplemented by evidence of more severe and long-term effects and this was consistent across the three locations.

Age

Earlier analysis conducted by the Costs of the Troubles suggested that age was a key variable in relation to exposure to violence. Indeed, early work suggested that this was a conflict conducted primarily by the young. Accordingly, it was important to analyse the different experiences of the Troubles by age. However, in general, one should be cautious about the cross-tabulations containing the age variable. For one thing, the Troubles have stretched over 30 years and were most intense in the first half of the 1970s. Individuals under 35 were not even alive then. Accordingly, those over 35 and particularly over 45 have had greater opportunity to experience the Troubles than those in the younger age groups. The earlier analysis was based on death statistics whenever they occurred. The results shown here are based on personal recollection of respondents. Older people simply have longer memories.

It should be noted that the stringent Chi-Square significance test (.005) excluded a very large number of crosstabulations based on age. Accordingly, the following analysis relates only to those tables were the age differences were judged to be significant at that level. The exclusion of a very large number of cross-tabulations on the grounds of lack of significant difference suggests even more caution in drawing conclusions.

Table 3.26 How Much Experience would you say you have of the Troubles?

	AGE:	15-19	20-24	25-39	40-59	60-64	65-79	80+	Total
A lot	Count	5	8	60	83	19	13	5	193
	% within Age	8.1	5.9	14.7	20.2	19.0	9.6	14.7	15.0
Quite a lot	Count	9	28	91	85	9	28	7	257
	% within Age	14.5	20.6	22.4	20.7	9.0	20.7	20.6	20.0
Some	Count	23	38	118	95	28	31	4	337
	% within Age	37.1	27.9	29.0	23.2	28.0	23.0	11.8	26.2
A little	Count	11	25	53	46	18	27	5	185
	% within Age	17.7	18.4	13.0	11.2	18.0	20.0	14.7	14.4
Very little	Count	12	34	80	83	24	30	11	274
	% within Age	19.4	25.0	19.7	20.2	24.0	22.2	32.4	21.3
None	Count	2	3	5	18	2	6	2	38
	% within Age	3.2	2.2	1.2	4.4	2.0	4.4	5.9	3.0
Total	Count	62	136	407	410	100	135	34	1284
	% within Age	100.0	100.0	100.0	100.0	100.0	100.0	100.0	100.0

The responses in Table 3.26 seem to question the hypothesis that younger age groups disproportionately experienced the Troubles. Of those reporting having 'a lot' of experience of the Troubles, (Question 37) the 45-64 age group had the highest percentages. This was also true of each of the three groups of wards. Indeed, almost 15 per cent of the 80+ group reported in this high category. However, the finding is complicated by the subjective interpretations involved. For a person in their 80s, 'a lot' may involve considerably less contact with violence than for a person in their 30s. If the three major categories (some, quite a lot and a lot) are aggregated, the 25-39 age group reported most experience of the Troubles. These patterns were consistent across the three locations.

Table 3.27   Can you tell me how often you have experienced straying into an area where you did not feel safe?

	AGE:	15-19	20-24	25-39	40-59	60-64	65-79	80+	Total
Very often	Count	4	9	46	46	7	7	2	121
	% within Age	6.6	6.5	11.3	11.1	7.0	5.1	6.1	9.4
Occas-ionally	Count	18	35	104	120	20	17	2	316
	% within Age	29.5	25.2	25.5	29.0	20.0	12.4	6.1	24.5
Seldom	Count	22	41	130	100	26	32	13	364
	% within Age	36.1	29.5	31.9	24.2	26.0	23.4	39.4	28.2
Never	Count	17	54	128	148	47	81	16	491
	% within Age	27.9	38.8	31.4	35.7	47.0	59.1	48.5	38.0
Total	Count	61	139	408	414	100	137	33	1292
	% within Age	100.0	100.0	100.0	100.0	100.0	100.0	100.0	100.0

A similar picture emerged with the question about the experience of straying into areas where the respondent did not feel safe (Table 3.27) Over ten per cent of the 25-39 age categories reported this experience a lot compared to just under seven per cent in the under 25 age groups. Almost 34 per cent of the entire sample reported having this experience 'very often or 'occasionally' compared to 40 per cent of the 40-59 age group, 36 per cent of the 15-19 and 32 per cent of the 20-24 age groups. It should be noted that the 40-59 age group was the most numerous within the sample.

Table 3.28 Can you tell me how often you have experienced being wary in the presence of people from the other community?

	AGE:	15-19	20-24	25-39	40-59	60-64	65-79	80+	Total
Very often	Count	8	18	59	63	9	5	1	163
	% within Age	12.9	13.0	14.5	15.1	8.9	3.6	3.0	12.6
Occas-ionally	Count	18	38	115	100	21	19	4	315
	% within Age	29.0	27.5	28.2	23.9	20.8	13.9	12.1	24.3
Seldom	Count	21	36	94	109	24	37	12	333
	% within Age	33.9	26.1	23.0	26.1	23.8	27.0	36.4	25.7
Never	Count	15	46	140	146	47	76	16	486
	% within Age	24.2	33.3	34.3	34.9	46.5	55.5	48.5	37.5
Total	Count	62	138	408	418	101	137	33	1297
	% within Age	100.0	100.0	100.0	100.0	100.0	100.0	100.0	100.0

The 40-59 age group also had the highest scores in reporting wariness in the presence of people from the other community. Just over 15 per cent reported this experience very often compared to 12.6 per cent in the general population and around 13 per cent of the under 25 group. However, if the 'occasionally' and 'very often' categories are aggregated, the 15-19 age group (41.9%) and the 25-39 group (42.7%) recorded the highest scores. Some small variations were noted between locations, but the small number of cases involved makes it inadvisable to draw firm conclusions from this variation.

Table 3.29 Can you tell me how often you have had to change normal routes, routines or habits because of safety?

	AGE:	15-19	20-24	25-39	40-59	60-64	65-79	80+	Total
Very often	Count	4	19	61	53	6	2	1	146
	% within Age	6.5	13.7	14.9	12.7	5.9	1.5	3.0	11.2
Occas-ionally	Count	6	13	55	57	16	9	1	157
	% within Age	9.7	9.4	13.4	13.6	15.8	6.6	3.0	12.1
Seldom	Count	11	24	66	54	12	23	4	194
	% within Age	17.7	17.3	16.4	12.9	11.9	16.9	12.1	14.9
Never	Count	41	83	227	254	67	102	27	801
	% within Age	66.1	59.7	55.5	60.8	66.3	75.0	81.8	61.7
Total	Count	62	139	409	418	101	136	33	1298
	% within Age	100.0	100.0	100.0	100.0	100.0	100.0	100.0	100.0

With regard to changing routines to ensure safety (Table 3.29), the 25-59 age groups again reported the most frequent experiences. 28.3 per cent of the former and 26.3 per cent of the latter reported changing routines either 'very often' or 'occasionally'. This compares to just over 16 per cent of the 15-19 group.

Table 3.30 shows that about a quarter of the sample had seen people killed or injured at least once. Interestingly, 37.1 per cent the youngest age group, the highest in the sample, reported this experience. Given the earlier discussed age bias in these findings, this is remarkable. This might point to experience of paramilitary punishments. Unfortunately the cross-tabulation to identify this possibility did not meet the strict confident level utilised in this analysis.

	AGE:	15-19	20-24	25-39	40-59	60-64	65-79	80+	Total
Several times	Count	2	1	21	22	4		1	51
	% within Age	3.2	0.7	5.1	5.3	4.0		3.1	3.9
More than once	Count	6	21	35	53	6	14	1	136
	% within Age	9.7	15.1	8.6	12.8	5.9	10.1	3.1	10.5
Once	Count	15	18	71	45	11	13		173
	% within Age	24.2	12.9	17.4	10.9	10.9	9.4		13.4
Never	Count	39	99	282	293	80	111	30	934
	% within Age	62.9	71.2	68.9	70.9	79.2	80.4	93.8	72.2
Total	Count	62	139	409	413	101	138	32	1294
	% within Age	100.0	100.0	100.0	100.0	100.0	100.0	100.0	100.0

Table 3.30   Can I ask if you have seen people being killed or physically injured?

Table 3.31 shows reported changes in drinking habits attributed to the Troubles. The 25-39 age group report both highest percentage of people reporting no change in their drinking and the highest percentage reporting an increase. The other marked difference between age groups is the high percentages of older people who have always abstained from alcohol (over 40% of all respondents over 65). No differences were noted in responses between the three locations.

Table 3.31   On balance, do you think your drinking has changed as a result of your experiences of the Troubles?

AGE:		15-19	20-24	25-39	40-59	60-64	65-79	80+	Total
No	Count	40	97	299	250	63	62	13	824
	% within Age	65.6	69.8	73.6	60.8	63.6	45.6	43.3	64.3
Yes in- creased	Count	3	14	54	49	4	3	2	131
	% within Age	8.2	10.1	13.3	11.9	4.0	2.2	6.7	10.2
Yes de- creased	Count	1	2	7	13	1	5		29
	% within Age	1.6	1.4	1.7	3.2	1.0	3.7		2.3
Always abstain- ed	Count	12	23	39	78	29	61	14	256
	% within Age	19.7	16.5	9.6	19.0	29.3	44.9	46.7	20.0
Abstain now	Count	3	3	7	21	2	5	1	42
	% within Age	4.9	2.2	1.7	5.1	2.0	3.7	3.3	3.3
Total	Count	61	139	406	411	99	136	30	1282
	% within Age	100.0	100.0	100.0	100.0	100.0	100.0	100.0	100.0

Because of the changing character of the Troubles over time, the personal experiences and, therefore, perceptions of them by different age groups vary. Accordingly, there must be some reservation about drawing conclusions based on the age differences of the respondents.

In addition, there is the issue of self-medication with drugs or alcohol to cope with Troubles' experiences. For example, just over 10 per cent of the 20-24 year olds claimed that their drinking had increased. Over 16 per cent indicated that there had been periods when they 'drank a lot after a particular experience' and almost half of these said that the period extended for more than six months. Again, almost a third of this group reported that the drinking had either 'severe' or 'moderate' interference with their lives. While these are small percentages relative to total sample size, they suggest, nevertheless, that sizeable numbers of the Northern Ireland population are similarly affected. The tendency to report increases in drinking was higher for all ages in high intensity locations, than in medium or low intensity locations.

Disability

The analysis of Troubles related experiences would not be complete without some reference to those suffering disability. Unfortunately, whilst the questionnaire asked about disability in general it did not contain a question that directly related to that condition to the Troubles as a causative factor. Within the sample 39 people reported that they had been injured in a bomb explosion at least once and 33 had been injured in shootings. A small number of each had suffered both. In total, there were 62 individuals with such injuries - about 4.5 per cent of the sample. This is dramatically higher than the ratio of 40,000 injured in the Troubles from a population of 1.5 million. A higher number reported health deterioration as the result of Troubles-related trauma or bereavement - 287 cases or just over a fifth of the total sample. Just fewer than six per cent of the sample (79 cases of whom 56 reported health deterioration) reported being given medication to kill pain for conditions that resulted from the Troubles. There were marked differences between the three locations, disability being highest in the high intensity locations.

Experience of the Troubles and the Impact on People's Lives

A crucial question for this study concerns the impact the Troubles have had on people's lives. In a post-conflict situation, an important concern is with victim support. How should those who have suffered most during the violent era be supported/compensated? There are also very different views about who properly constitute victims. The Costs of the Troubles project has made clear elsewhere the criteria by which it has defined victims (see Fay, Morrissey and Smyth, 1999). However, equally important questions concern the characteristics of those who suffered most and what impact it has had on their lives.

It is reasonable to ask first about the relationship between experience of the Troubles and the impact on people's lives. The natural assumption is that the higher the degree of experience, the greater will be the impact. However, this cannot be assumed. People respond to trauma in different ways. Other social and community factors mediate the impact of encounters with the various phenomena of the Troubles. To explore this issue, the responses to the question about experiences of the Troubles was crosstabulated with those about the impact on people' lives.

Table 3.32 Experience of the Troubles by the Change in People's Lives

	A lot	Quite a lot	Some	A little	Very little	None	Total	Number
complete change	3.7	3.1	0.5	0.1	0.1	0.1	7.5	99
radical change	2.8	2.7	2.2	0.5	0.6		8.8	116
some change	6.6	10.0	13.2	5.1	4.0	0.1	39.1	514
small impact	1.5	3.3	9.7	7.8	11.7	1.4	35.3	465
not at all	0.4	0.4	1.3	1.4	4.6	1.2	9.3	122
Total	15.0	19.5	26.8	14.9	21.0	2.7	100.0	1316
Number	198	256	353	196	277	36	1316	

Other than the rows and columns containing actual numbers, the figures in the table are percentages of the entire sample. Thus, 3.7 per cent of the whole sample responded by declaring both that they had 'a lot' of experience of the Troubles and it 'completely changed' their lives.   Interestingly, of those experiencing the Troubles 'a lot', 'quite a lot' or 'some', the common response on impact was 'some change'. Of the 198 who experienced the Troubles 'a lot', just under half indicated 'some change' in their lives compared to just over a fifth who declared a complete change. Half of those each reporting 'quite a lot' and 'some' indicated 'some change' compared to less than a sixth and less than a fiftieth expressing complete change respectively. It would thus appear that the relationship between experience and impact on one's life is not linear.

The diagram below points to the complexity of the relationship. The categories that reflect the most extensive experience of the Troubles have their maximum points at 'some change'. The remaining three low-experience clusters have their maximum points at 'small impact'. There was thus a tendency for all categories of experience to report 'change' in their lives. This, however, was concentrated in just two of the impact categories. It may well be that self-reporting systems as employed in this survey will not elucidate responses at the extreme end of the scale.

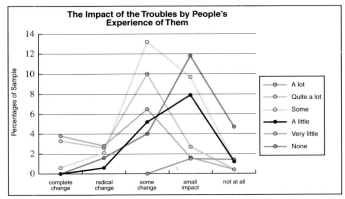

The Impact of the Troubles by People's Experience of Them

However, it would be unwise to conclude that the totality of the relationship between experiencing the Troubles and their impact on people could be encapsulated by a single crosstabulation. To explore the issue further, three exercises were undertaken:

* The first was to develop an indicator for the existence of post-traumatic stress and to explore the characteristics of those in the sample in whom it was detected. As will be detailed later, this was not an exercise in clinical diagnosis but was based on answers provided in a questionnaire. Nevertheless, the task in hand is research rather than treatment and there is thus a value in exploring the issue;

* The second was to develop indicators to identify those who had 'severe' and 'very severe' experiences of the Troubles and those for whom the Troubles had 'severe and 'very severe' impact (The same cautions apply to these as for the indicator of post-traumatic stress) and to examine their characteristics.

* The third was to test for relationships between the experience and impact variables.

A Post Traumatic Stress Indicator

Thus, a measure was constructed, loosely based on the diagnostic criteria for Post Traumatic Stress Disorder. Both the International Classification of Diseases (ICD 10) and the

Diagnostic and Statistical Manual of Mental Disorders (DSM-IV) set out diagnostic criteria for Post Traumatic Stress Disorder. The latter was used as a basis for this exercise. The criteria set out in the DSM-IV are as follows:

A. The person has been exposed to a traumatic event in which the person experienced, witnessed or was confronted with an event or events that involved actual or threatened death or serious injury or a threat to the physical integrity of self or others, and the person's response involved intense fear, helplessness or horror.

B. The traumatic event is persistently re-experienced in one (or more) of the following ways:

1. Recurrent and intrusive distressing recollections of the event, including images thoughts or perceptions.

2. Recurrent distressing dreams of the event

3. Acting or feeling as if the traumatic event were recurring (includes dissociative flashback episodes, including those that occur on awakening or when intoxicated

4. Intense psychological distress at exposure to internal or external cues that symbolise or represent an aspect of the traumatic event.

5. Physiological reactivity on exposure to internal or external cues that symbolize or resemble an aspect of the traumatic event.

C. Persistent avoidance of stimuli associated with the trauma and numbing of general responsiveness (not present before the trauma) as indicated by three or more of the following:

1. efforts to avoid thoughts, feelings or conversations associated with the trauma

2. efforts to avoid activities, places, or people that arouse recollections of the trauma

3. inability to recall an important aspect of the trauma

4. markedly diminished interest or participation in significant activities

5. feelings of detachment or estrangement from others

6. restricted range of affect (e.g. unable to have loving feelings)

7. sense of a foreshortened future (e.g. does not expect to have a career, marriage, children or a normal life span)

D. Persistent symptoms of increased arousal (not present before the trauma) as indicated by two or more of the following:

1. difficulty falling or staying asleep

2. irritability or outbursts of anger

3. difficulty concentrating

4. hypervigilance
5. exaggerated startle response

E. Duration of the disturbance is more than 1 month

F. The disturbance causes clinically significant distress or impairment in social, occupational or other important areas of functioning. (source: DSM-IV: American Psychiatric Association)

Clearly it is not possible (clinically) to arrive at a diagnosis of Port Traumatic Stress Disorder without conducting a proper clinical interview. Therefore, this exercise that we have embarked on can only be seen as the loosest of indicators of the stress levels in the sampled population. Our questionnaire did not exactly measure the criteria as set out in the DSM-IV, but we constructed a measure of Traumatic Stress based on the following responses to the questionnaire

Exposure to a traumatic event: positive response to one of the following questions in the questionnaire:

47: *Have you ever had a period of time when you kept having painful memories of your experience/s even when you tried not to think about it?* [frequently/occasionally/ rarely/never/ don't remember]

48: Have you ever had a period of time when you had repeated dreams and nightmares about your experience/s? [frequently/occasionally/ rarely/never/ don't remember]

49: Have you ever had a period of time when you found yourself in a situation which made you feel as though it was happening all over again? [frequently/occasionally/ rarely/never/ don't remember]

and **63a: Do you agree that the Troubles have caused me a great deal of distress and emotional upset?** [Strongly agree/ Agree/Neither agree nor disagree/ Disagree/ Strongly disagree]

Re-experiencing the traumatic event: positive response to three of the following questions in the questionnaire:

Questions

64j: Do you agree/ disagree that the Troubles have made members of my family and/or me seriously consider emigration? [strongly agree/agree/neither agree nor disagree/disgree/strongly disagree]

65d: Do you agree/disagree that the Troubles have restricted the number of areas I am prepared to go into for work? [strongly agree/agree/ neither agree nor disagree/ disagree/ strongly disagree]

50: Have you ever had a period of time when you lost interest in activities that had meant a lot to you before? [frequently/ occasionally/ rarely/never/ don't remember]

67a: In general, would you agree/disagree that the Troubles have nothing to do with me? [strongly agree/agree/ neither agree nor disagree/ disagree/ strongly disagree]

63a: Do you agree/ disagree that the Troubles have caused me a great deal of distress and emotional upset? [strongly agree/agree/ neither agree nor disagree/ disagree/ strongly disagree]

and **63f: Do you agree/ disagree that the Troubles have shattered my illusion that the world is a safe place?** [strongly agree/agree/ neither agree nor disagree/ disagree/ strongly disagree]

Persistent symptoms of increased arousal: positive response to two of the following questions in the questionnaire:

Questions

52: Have you ever had a period of difficulty sleeping due to your experiences of the Troubles? [frequently/occasionally/rarely/ never/don't remember]

63e: Do you agree/disagree that the Troubles have provoked strong feelings of rage in me? [strongly agree/agree/ neither agree nor disagree/ disagree/ strongly disagree]

29: During the past 4 weeks have you had any of the following problems with your work or other regular daily activities as a result of any emotional problem (such as feeling depressed or anxious)? - Didn't do work or other activities as carefully as usual? [Yes/No]

64l: Do you agree/disagree that the Troubles have made me extremely fearful for my own and my family's safety? [strongly agree/agree/ neither agree nor disagree/ disagree/ strongly disagree]

51: Have you ever had a period of time when you were very jumpy or more easily startled than usual or felt that you had to be on your guard all the time? [frequently/occasionally/ rarely/never/ don't remember]

and *53: Have there been times when you felt ashamed or guilty about surviving events in the Troubles?* [frequently/occasionally/ rarely/never/ don't remember]

Thus, those who have met these criteria have been exposed to a highly stressful event and report a range of symptoms of traumatic stress, as measured by the specified questions.

When the PTS indicator was constructed, it applied to 390 cases, about 30 per cent of the entire sample. This might seem overly large although the existence of the group of high intensity wards contributed to the high number. It was crosstabulated with other variables to determine the characteristics of those who 'fitted' the condition. Interestingly, there were only small differences between men (30%) and women (28%) despite the different nature of their experiences of the Troubles. In the original analysis of the deaths' database, women were fewer than 10 per cent of the total. The survey material suggested that men and women tended to have different kinds of experience of the Troubles but that women were much more affected than indicated by the deaths' database analysis. This variable applies

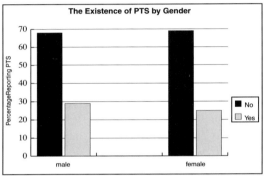

a single standard to both genders and indicates very similar percentages that have been affected in this way. Women are thus moved more to the centre of the analysis of victims than was previously the case.

At the same time, significant differences emerged when the PTS indicator was crosstabulated with religion and location.

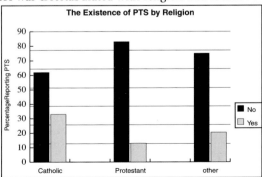

A higher percentage of Catholics were affected by PTS compared to Protestants. This is entirely in keeping with other survey findings, particularly the greater range and intensity of Catholic experience of the Troubles. Clearly, it can be suggested that the primary axis of the conflict was the republican campaign for a United Ireland. The source of the conflict was thus Catholic areas, which saw at least four strands of violent activity:

* Republican paramilitaries against the security forces and vice versa, including the 'unintended' casualties of both;
* In some areas, Catholic victims of Loyalist paramilitaries;
* Internal feuds amongst Republican paramilitaries;
* Internal 'policing' by Republican paramilitaries.

It is the existence of all four strands that made the Catholic experience of the Troubles that much more extensive. This does not detract from the disproportionate PTS effect. The differences by religion are mirrored in differences amongst areas.

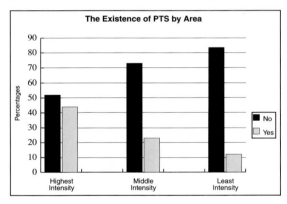

The group of wards selected because they had highest death rates also had the highest incidence of the PTS indicator. Although the variable was constructed without regard to location, almost half (45%) of respondents from such wards showed evidence of PTS.

When the PTS indicator was crosstabulated with question 71 (how much your experiences of the Troubles have affected you?), the following pattern emerged.

Table 3.33 PTS and Overall Impact of the Troubles		No	Yes
complete change		9	90
	%	9.1	90.9
radical change		52	67
	%	43.7	56.3
some change		345	176
	%	66.2	33.8
small impact		426	48
	%	89.9	10.1
not at all		115	7
	%	94.3	5.7
Total		947	388
	%	70.9	29.1

Of those who reported a 'complete change' in their lives, just over 90 per cent showed evidence of PTS while over two thirds of those reporting 'radical change' were similarly affected. At the other end of the scale, just over five per cent of those whom the Troubles affected 'not at all' indicated PTS. It should be noted that over 15 per cent of the sample reported a 'complete change' or 'radical change' in their lives as a result of the Troubles. The high intensity wards heavily influenced this figure. But, if this condition were only one third as prevalent in the general population, then 75,000 people would be affected.

SF12 Analysis

In addition to seeking information about the respondents' experience of the Troubles and their effects, it was decided to apply a standard health measure - Short Form 12 (SF12). SF12 is 'a multipurpose short-form generic measure of health status. It was developed to be a much shorter, yet valid alternative to the SF36 for use in large surveys of general and specific populations'.[1] Because of the very large number of variables in the survey, SF12 was regarded as preferably to SF36 (of which it is a subset) because of its brevity.

Respondents were asked to answer a series of questions about their general health, their capacity to engage in a range of

---

[1] Ware, J.E., Kosinski, M. and Keller, S. (1995), SF-12: How to Score the SF-12 Physical and Mental Health Summary Scales, New England Medical Center, Boston, p.11.

activities, their experience of pain and feelings of calm, energy and depression. Scores on these questions are weighted and rationalised to produce eight scales that, in turn, can be used to generate two summary measures:

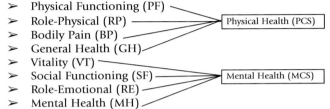

- ➢ Physical Functioning (PF)
- ➢ Role-Physical (RP)
- ➢ Bodily Pain (BP)
- ➢ General Health (GH)

Physical Health (PCS)

- ➢ Vitality (VT)
- ➢ Social Functioning (SF)
- ➢ Role-Emotional (RE)
- ➢ Mental Health (MH)

Mental Health (MCS)

Across these scales, higher scores reflected better health. The primary interest lay in comparing SF12 scores across the three sets of wards. It was assumed that since physical health deteriorates with age, it would be important to compare each of the age bands in each ward set. However, three-way crosstabulation for the SF12 scales, Location and the Age01 variable proved to have unacceptably high Chi Sq. scores (higher than the low significance level of .05). Different SF12 scores across the age bands might therefore have been random rather than systematic. Accordingly, it was decided simply to compare the mean scores for each SF12 scale for each area. These are described in table (3.34).

Table 3.34 SF12 Scales	High Intensity Wards		Medium Intensity Wards		Low Intensity Wards	
	Mean	Std. Dev	Mean	Std. Dev	Mean	Std. Dev
General Health	3.3	1.3	3.6	1.2	3.7	1.1
Physical Functioning	5.1	1.4	5.2	1.4	5.3	1.2
Role-Physical	3.4	0.9	3.6	0.8	3.6	0.8
Bodily Pain	4.8	1.7	5.1	1.5	5.4	1.2
VITALITY	3.7	1.6	4.1	1.5	4.0	1.4
Mental Health	5.9	1.5	6.4	1.3	6.4	1.1
Social Functioning	3.9	1.3	4.3	1.2	4.4	1.0
Role Emotional	3.5	0.9	3.7	0.7	3.7	0.7

Both means and standard deviations on these eight scales are remarkably similar across all three locations. However, respondents living in high intensity wards had consistently the lowest scores on all eight scales. In most cases the differences were marginal (ranging from .2 to .6 on physical variables .2 to .5 on mental health variables) but systematic.

Support

• Respondents reported that most of their support came from their immediate family, and those who sought outside support from statutory were most likely to seek it from their GP. However, with this exception, respondents were much more likely to look to the voluntary sector for help than to professional sources.

A relevant question is about the form of support individuals with evidence of PTS received. Table 3.35 describes the percentage of those indicating PTS who received support from the following sources.

Table 3.35   Sources of Support for Those With Evidence of PTS

	Percentage of All with PTS
Statutory	
Psychiatrist	14%
Clinical Psychologist	4%
GP and Local Doctor	49%
Community Nurse	17%
Social Worker	11%
Non-Statutory	
Minister or Priest	20%
Community Worker	25%
Other Voluntary Organisation	20%

Within the statutory sector, GPs bear the main responsibility for support with almost half. Interestingly, non-statutory helpers have given support to a higher percentage of the group than any other statutory professional. The important role of the community sector in this regard should also be noted.

In general, there was satisfaction with the support received. Just over half described the help as both 'sympathetic and helpful' with another 15 per cent describing it as adequate. Only six cases described the help as 'harmful'. At the same time, when asked - 'where, if from anywhere, did you receive the best help?' - just over two thirds indicated a combination of spouse, family and neighbours. It would thus appear that informal welfare systems had the primary role. 34 cases reported that they had appropriate help from no one. Some differences emerge between high, medium and low intensity areas in terms of sources and evaluation of help, and these were discussed earlier (see Appendix 4).

Severe and Very Severe Experiences of the Troubles

It was decided to examine those in the sample who had the most intense experience of the Troubles. For that purpose, two new variables were constructed. The first was designed to capture 'severe' experiences. Five key events were identified:
*   Being close to a bomb explosion;
*   Witnessing a shooting;
*   Having a neighbour killed;
*   Seeing people killed or seriously injured, and;
*   Having to leave home permanently.
Some of these may overlap - for example, a neighbour may have been killed in a bomb explosion. Accordingly, the criterion used to identify 'severe' experiences was having been exposed to at least three of these events.
For 'very severe' experiences, seven events prioritised:
*   Having a close friend killed;
*   Being physically attacked due to the Troubles;
*   Being injured in a bomb explosion;
*   Being injured in a shooting;
*   Having a member of the immediate family injured;
*   Having a member of the immediate family killed;
*   Having another relative killed.
Given the seriousness of these events and the fact that they overlap less than the variable above, the condition specified for 'very severe' experiences of the Troubles was exposure to any two of these events.

The variable 'severe experience' affected 123 cases within the sample, just less than 10 per cent of the total. It was more characteristic of men (11.2%) than women (7.3%), of Catholics (12.3%) than Protestants (2.3%) and of the high intensity wards (19.5% compared to 5.1% and 1.7% respectively).

Almost a third of those who had a severe experience of the Troubles reported that the Troubles had 'completely changed my life'. A further 18 per cent claimed a radical change. Thus for around half the group (48%), the Troubles have had significant impact. A further two fifths reported 'some changes' to their lives.

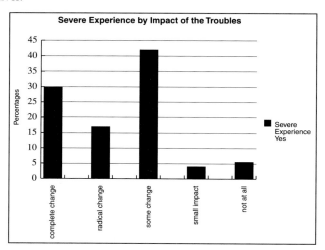

The group identified as having 'very severe' experiences of the Troubles numbered 208 of which 56 per cent were male and 44 per cent female. It was 84 per cent Catholic and 62 per cent lived in the high intensity wards. Two fifths of this group reported a 'complete' or 'radical' change in their lives as a result of the Troubles and another 44 per cent reported some change. Less than a fifth suggested that the Troubles had only a 'small' or 'no' impact on their lives.

The severe and very severe experience groups had 56 members in common.

Severe and Very Severe Impact

Two similar variables were constructed as indicators of the Troubles' impact. The first (severe impact) was based on the Troubles:

* Caused me a great deal of distress and emotional upset;
* Made violence more a part of my life;
* Left me feeling helpless;
* Provoked strong feelings of range in me.

Severe impact was said to apply when, on at least two conditions, respondents either strongly agreed or agreed.

Very severe impact employed a different set of conditions. The Troubles have:

* Completely ruined my life;
* Damaged my health;
* Caused me to lose loved ones through death;
* Physically damaged me/my family.

Because of the stark nature of these conditions, very severe impact was said to have occurred when respondents either strongly agreed or agreed to any.

The severe impact variable applied to 232 cases. Just over 18 per cent of women (131 cases) compared to 16 per cent of men (100) cases were identified as suffering severe impact - over a fifth of Catholics, compared to less than a twelfth of Protestants - more than half of those with severe impact inhabited wards (over a quarter of the people living in such wards) which had had the highest intensity of violence. Over 80 per cent of these individuals also showed evidence of PTS.

For the very severe impact variable, there were 252 cases. These made up almost 20 per cent of men and almost 18 per cent of women - just less than a quarter of Catholics in the sample and less than an eighth of Protestants - a third of the population of high intensity wards compared to less than a tenth of the population of least intensity wards.

Almost 45 per cent of those suffering severe impact and 53 per cent of those suffering very severe impact declared that the Troubles had 'completely' or 'radically' changed their lives. In each, a further third indicated 'some changes'.

The next table summaries the forms of support received by each group, their respective assessment of that support and the sources from which they had the 'best' help.

Table 3.36 Summary of Support for those with Severe Impact and Very Severe Impact	Severe Impact	Very Severe Impact
% who received support from:		
Psychiatrist	15%	19.8%
Clinical psychologist	4%	4%
GP/local doctor	50.3%	62.2%
Community nurse	22%	24.6%
Social worker	12%	14%
Minister/priest	19.2%	26.1%
Community worker	26.8%	28.2%
Voluntary Organisation	24.3%	23.7%
% regarding the support as sympathetic & helpful	51.8%	60.1%
Source of best help		
Spouse	24.6%	24.8%
Parents	17.9%	16.2%
Other close family	17.4%	20.3%
Close friends	7.2%	9.9%
Local Doctor	2.1%	4.1%

The pattern is familiar from the analysis of PTS. Doctors are the primary source of support within the statutory system. Other more specialised professionals are involved to a substantially less extent. Priests/ministers have been a greater source of support to the very severe rather than the severe category, presumably because some of the former's defining conditions were associated with death. The role of the community sector is highlighted, as is the informal welfare systems of family and friends.

There are two striking points about the analysis of experience and impact:

* Apparently the percentages of the sample suffering severe impacts are greater than those relating to severe experiences. However, all four variables are constructs and the different numbers thrown up are partly a result of decisions about the number and combination of defining conditions;

* Gender differences are very minimal indeed, particularly with the impact variables. This is in spite of considerable differences in the death rate and in other experiences of the Troubles between males and females.

Conclusion

Effects of the Troubles

- Of those reporting painful memories, over a third of respondents came from the wards with the highest intensity of violence compared to a fifth from the wards in the middle intensity group;

- An eighth of those from middle intensity wards compared to over a quarter from wards in the highest intensity group reported nightmares and dreams related to the Troubles;

- In highest intensity wards involuntary recall was reported by a third of respondents compared to an eighth of respondents in the middle intensity wards;

- 30 per cent of those from the highest intensity wards compared to just 11 per cent in the middle intensity group reported some form of guilt at surviving;

- Just over four per cent of those from middle intensity wards, whereas 22 per cent from highest intensity wards reported an increase in alcohol assumption related to the Troubles;

- More severe experience and severe effects of the Troubles were reported by those in the highest intensity wards than those in the other two locations;

- More health problems were reported by those in high intensity wards than by those in the other two locations;

Help and support with the effects of the Troubles

- Help was sought more frequently from those in wards of highest intensity compared to those in the middle and low intensity wards;

- Respondents in all three groups reported that the primary source of help was from immediate family and friends, although, between the three locations there were differences reported in help sought outside the family network;

- Of those who did seek help, over 40 per cent in the high intensity group claimed they were unable to find adequate help, compared to 29 per cent in both middle and low intensity wards;

- The belief that nothing could help was reported by over 83 per cent in the highest intensity wards compared to over 12 per cent in the low intensity wards and just over 4 per cent in the middle intensity wards;

- When asked about medication, almost a quarter from the highest intensity wards reported that they had taken some from of medication, compared to just under an eighth in the middle intensity wards and just over 9 per cent in wards with low intensity violence;

- 52 per cent of those who used medication in highest intensity wards reported that they were on medication permanently compared to 35 per cent of those who use medication in low intensity wards and just over 9 per cent in the middle intensity group;

- In the highest intensity wards medication was used for anti-depression, sleep disturbance or sedation purposes. In the low intensity wards however medication was used for pain control rather than anti-depressive purposes;

Segregation

- Those living in segregated areas were four times more likely to report 'a lot' of experience of the Troubles than those in non-segregated areas. Twice as many residents of segregated as opposed to non-segregated areas reported 'quite a lot' of experience of the Troubles;

- Over a fifth of those in segregated areas reported a complete or radical change due to the Troubles, compared to a twelfth in non-segregated areas;

Gender

- A higher proportion of men (37.5%) than women (22.3%) report 'a lot' or 'quite a lot' of experience of the Troubles with a fifth of men and a quarter of women reporting little or no experience;

- Some experiences were shared by both men and women whilst some more direct experiences - being called sectarian names, or getting into physical fights or witnessing a shooting - are more frequently encountered by men. Similar percentages reported death or injury in their immediate families;

Religion

- The percentage of Catholics reporting a lot (18.9%) and quite a lot (22.8%) of experience of the Troubles was much higher than that of Protestants (5.25% and 13.8% respectively) whilst only 15% of Catholics compared to 38.9% of Protestants reported very little experience of the Troubles. We conclude that Catholic experience of the Troubles is disproportionately high;

- Of those reporting a complete change in their lives due to the Troubles, 90.9% were Catholic compared to 8.1% Protestant, and Catholics overall report having experienced more extreme effects of the Troubles, whereas Protestants report less overall change on a smaller scale;

- In spite of this, proportionately more Protestants than Catholics reported long-standing illnesses;

- Catholics reported more painful memories of the Troubles, dreams and nightmares about the Troubles, intrusive thoughts, losing interest in normal activities and feelings of insecurity and jumpiness than Protestants;

Age

- The 45-64 age group had the highest percentages of people reporting 'a lot' of experience of the Troubles, and the 40-59 age group reported more experience of straying into areas where they did not feel safe and more experience of feeling wary in the presence of the 'other' community compared to other age groups;

- About a quarter of the sample had seen people killed or injured at least once, with 37.1% of 15-19 year olds - the highest rate for any age group - reporting this experience;

Alcohol use related to the Troubles

- The 25-39 age group contained the highest percentage of those reporting no change in their drinking and the highest percentage reporting an increase, with no difference emerging between the three locations in this question;

- However, over 10% of 20-24 year olds reported that their drinking had increased, and 16% said that at times they 'drank a lot after a particular experience' and almost half ot hose said that the period lasted for more than six months;

Experience of the Troubles

* About 4.5% of the sample reported that they had been injured in a bomb explosion or in shootings;

Health

- Over a fifth of the total sample reported deterioration in their health which they attributed to a Troubles-related trauma or bereavement;
- Just less than 6% reported being given pain medication to treat conditions they suffered as a result of the effects of the Troubles on them;
- Analysis of the standard health measure (SF12) revealed remarkably little variation between the three locations. These results will be subjected to further analysis;

Experience of the Troubles and effects of the Troubles

- A complex relationship between experience of the Troubles and the reported effects of the Troubles was found. Whilst the majority of those who reported experience of the Troubles reported 'some change' in their lives, whilst relatively few in all categories including those with 'a lot' of experience reported 'complete change' in their lives due to the Troubles;
- A sub-group of the sample who reported severe and very severe experiences of the Troubles were further analysed. Almost half of this group reported a significant of the Troubles on them. About a third of them reported that the Troubles had 'completely changed my life,' and a further 18% reported a radical change. This sub-group was 84% Catholic and 62% lived in high intensity wards;
- A further sub-group who reported severe impact of the

Troubles were further analysed. Over half of this group lived in high intensity wards, and accounted for a quarter of the total sample from such wards. Over 80% of this group met the criteria for inclusion on the post traumatic stress indicator;

Indications of post traumatic stress

- An indicator of post traumatic stress was constructed and revealed
- minimal differences between men and women's scores
- significant differences between Catholics and Protestants, with Catholics scoring higher on the indicator than Protestants
- significant differences between the three locations, with areas of high intensity violence scoring higher than medium intensity areas, which in turn scored higher than the low intensity areas
- those reporting complete change in their lives due to the Troubles scored higher on the indicator than any other category;

Indeed for every 'effects' variable, differences of this order are observable. Differential experience and effects of the Troubles would seem to be conditioned more by location than either gender or religion. These responses suggest that there have been three key dimensions to life in the areas most affected by the Troubles:

- first, there is the much greater exposure to Troubles-related events both from paramilitary organisations and the security forces - a set of experiences almost unmatched in the rest of Northern Ireland (this group of wards regularly reported experience of Troubles' related activity at twice the rate for middle wards and four times the rate for least intensity wards);
- second, there are insecurities and fears in being outside one's own area and an acute wariness of outsiders, for example reflected in efforts to conceal where one lives;
- third there is a strong pattern of segregation - over a quarter of those from highest intensity wards who were employed, worked only with members of their own community.

Of the five variables identified as being potentially significant in being associated with both different experiences and effects of the Troubles, location and religion stand out. Indeed these are connected, given the high degree of spatial polarisation in the form of sectarian segregation in Northern Ireland, which is exacerbated in those areas where Troubles-related violence has been most pervasive. As indicated earlier, the sampling procedure was weighted to 'over-represent' those areas where death rates were highest. Unsurprisingly, the most intensive and pervasive experiences of the Troubles occurred here. Nevertheless, like many social phenomena, the pattern of violence in Northern Ireland has been extremely uneven.

The analysis of the five variables above suggests the following set of relationships.

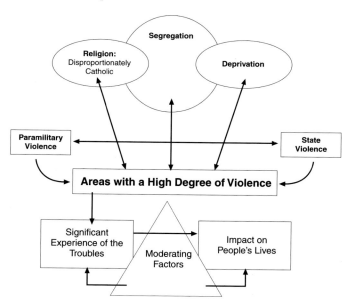

Recommendations

These factors should be recognised both in developing and delivering compensatory policies as part of any peace settlement. The spatial distribution of the impact of the Troubles, and its particular effects on sub-sections of the population should be part of the considerations of service planners and providers. Moreover, this concentrated experience of violence should figure in the operationalisation of New Targeting Social Need.

In certain areas, the experience of violence has been collective and multidimensional (local paramilitaries, paramilitaries from the 'other side' and the security forces have all contributed). Consequently, it makes sense to think in terms of spatially targeted programmes both to alleviate the effects and to emphasise the targeting of social and economic reconstruction. Consideration must also be given to the impact of such concentration on local cultures, expectations and attitudes. Community programmes aimed at areas worst affected which assess local need, raise expectations and provide information and support for local problem solving might offer a fruitful beginning for some of these areas.

The particular role of families and social support networks in helping those affected by the Troubles, and consideration should be given to how this can best be supported and recognised. Clearly, most people do not seek professional help for the effects of the Troubles on them, and of those who have had help, the majority report immediate family as its best and most accessible source.

Beyond the immediate family, the importance of the voluntary and community sector, and general practitioners in the provision of help from outside the family also emerges from the findings of this study. The prevalence of the use of alcohol and prescribed medication as means of coping with the Troubles, particularly amongst those worst affected also emerges, and an examination of alternatives to the use of drugs and alcohol might be a fruitful avenue for exploration by service providers.

Evaluation and Directions for future work

This survey, was part of a larger study aimed at elucidating the experience and effects of the Troubles on people in Northern Ireland. We hope it provides a useful base-line and starting point for other work in this field. We are aware of a numbre of areas for further exploration.

Standard health measures

Although we embedded a standard health measure (SF12) in the questionnaire, we have completed only a preliminary analysis of this here, due to difficulties in finding scores for the population for analysis purposes. In some ways we regret the choice of this instrument, since it has not been widely used (or used at all) in Northern Ireland, thus rendering our task of analysis more difficult. However, we will publish further analysis on this issue in future papers.

Inclusion of Questions on Stress

A second regret is that, in the process of editing the questionnaire, some of the questions designed to reflect the diagnostic criteria of the DSM-IV became edited and some were omitted altogether, requiring us to use less exact questions in the constructing of our Stress Indicator.

Finally, the survey has relied on interviewees reporting their memories of their experiences of the Troubles and their own assessment of the impact on them. The issue of the reliability of memory, and the issue of denial, which has been widely used in Northern Ireland and elsewhere as a coping mechanism in times of barely tolerable stress is also worth mentioning.

This survey can only report on what respondents remember, and what they do not now deny. Perhaps assessing the experience and the impact of events as terrible as armed conflict must always be an exercise in sailing among icebergs, where the danger of collision with what is not perceived makes us constantly nervous of shipwreck. We present this study with due nervousness, in the hope that it offers some useful insights and points of departure for our own and others' further work.

References

Bell, P., Kee, G., Loughrey, R., Roddy, R.J., and Curran, P.S. (1988) "Post Traumatic Stress in Northern Ireland." Acta Psychiatr. Scand. 77: 166-169.

Curran, P.S., Bell, P., Murray, A., Roddy, R., and Rocke, L.G. (1990) "Psychological Consequences of the Enniskillen Bombing." British Journal of Psychiatry: 156: 479-482.

Diagnostic and Statistical Manual of the American Psychiatric Association. Fourth edition.

Fay, M.T., Morrissey, M., and Smyth, M. (1998) Northern Ireland's Troubles: The Human Costs. London: Pluto.

Fraser, R.M., (1971) "The Cost of Commotion: An Analysis of the Psychiatric Sequelae of the 1969 Belfast Riots." Brit. J. Psychiat. (1971) 11, 237-64.

Fraser, R.M., Overy, R. Russell, J. Dunlap, R. and Bourne R. (1972) "Children and Conflict." Community Forum No 2 1972. Belfast: Community Relations Commission.

Lyons, H.A.(1974) "Terrorists' Bombing and the Psychological Sequelae." Journal of the Irish Medical Association. January 12, 1974. Vol 67, No 1.

Sutton, M. (1994) An Index of Deaths from the Conflict in Ireland 1969-1993. Belfast: Beyond the Pale.

World Health Organisation: International Classification of Diseases: Tenth edition.

Date of interview __/__/__

COST OF THE TROUBLES SURVEY

Questionnaire serial number _____

Ward code_____   **Interviewer code**_____

Before starting the interview:

"Cost of the Troubles" wrote to you about taking part in the survey it is carrying out into the effects of the troubles on people right across Northern Ireland.

You will have received a letter from us and a leaflet explaining the aims of our work. You may remember that we aim to establish the extent to which the troubles have affected people in all sections of the community, with a view to improving public understanding and services to people affected in various ways. We believe our work is worthwhile and important, and we hope you agree. We would be grateful for your participation in the survey. It is important that you participate, no matter how much or how little experience you have of the troubles.

All the information you may give me will be treated in strictest confidence, and I will not write down your name or other identifying details.

Some of the questions ask about experiences which are distressing. The questions ask about your experience of the troubles and are not intended to be intrusive. However, you may need to think about whether you wish to go ahead. I will listen sensitively and sympathetically. Some people have found that they felt better after talking about their experiences. If you want, I can also give you an advice leaflet and the names and phone numbers of helping organisations which work in this field, if you wish to get in touch with them. The decision to go ahead is yours and I would greatly appreciate it if you would add your experiences to our study. We wish to have a wide range of views and experiences included in our survey, and we would like you to be part of it.

COMPLETE ALL ITEMS - ONLY LEAVE BLANK IN THE EVENT
OF A REFUSAL OR WHERE THE RESPONDENT IS DIRECTED
AWAY FROM THE ITEM

SECTION A: HOUSEHOLD

1 How many people, including **Male**   **Female**   **Total**
   you, are there in the household?
   (Complete all cells. If there is no
   one in a particular category
   write "0")

   ____   ____   ____

2 How many including you   **Male**   **Female**   **Total**
   are aged: (Complete all cells)

		Male	Female	Total
(a)	0-4	....	....	....
(b)	5-9	....	....	....
(c)	10-14	....	....	....
(d)	15-19	....	....	....
(e)	20-24	....	....	....
(f)	25-39	....	....	....
(g)	40-59	....	....	....
(h)	60-64	....	....	....
(i)	65-79	....	....	....
(j)	80+	....	....	....

3 What is your age?   ....

4 Are you:

   male   1

   female   2

5 How many in the household are? <u>Male</u> <u>Female</u> <u>Total</u>
   (Complete all cells)

(a)   Married   .... |..........|...........

(b)   Single   .... |..........|...........

(c)   Widowed   .... |..........|...........

(d)   Single parents   .... |..........|...........

(e)   Separated/divorced   .... |..........|...........

6 Are you   Married   1

                    Single   2

                    Widowed   3

                    Single parents   4

                    Separated/divorced   5

7 How many in the household   <u>Male</u> <u>Female</u> <u>Total</u>
   including you are..?
   (Complete all cells)

(a)   In full-time or part-time   .... |..........|...........
        employment

(b)   On benefits   .... |..........|...........

(c)   At school   .... |..........|...........

(d)   In full-time or part-time   .... |..........|...........
        continuing/higher education

**8 What is the highest level of educational qualifications you
have gained?**

None	1
CSE/ NVQ	2
'O' Level/ GCSE	3
'A' Level/ B-Tech	4
Undergraduate degree	5
Postgraduate degree	6
Professional qualification	7
Other	8

SECTION B: TENURE & HOUSING

9   What type of accommodation is occupied by this household?

A caravan or other mobile or temporary structure	1
A whole house or bungalow that is a detached house	2
A whole house or bungalow that is semi-detached	3
A whole house or bungalow that is terraced/ include end of terrace	4
The whole of a purpose built flat or maisonette in a commercial building (eg in an office building or hotel or over a shop)	5
The whole of a purpose built flat or maisonette in a block of flats	6
Part of a converted or shared house, bungalow or flat with a separate entrance into the building	7
Part of a converted or shared house, bungalow or flat with a shared entrance into the building	8

10   Which of the following best describes your home?

Part of a current or former Housing Executive/public housing estate or development in a town or city setting	1
Part of a current or former Housing Executive/public housing estate or development in a rural setting	2
Part of a sheltered housing development in a town or city setting	3
Rural/isolated setting	4
Publicly owned house/flat in a village	5
In a private development	6
Not part of an estate or development	7
Don't Know/No response	8
Other	9

11   What type of tenure is your home?

rented	1
owned	2
Co-ownership	3

12 Housing segregation is widespread in Northern Ireland.
    Do you see the area you live in as segregated?
    yes   1
    no   2

SECTION C: OCCUPATION / WORK

*INTERVIEWER INSTRUCTIONS: the interviewees definition of
work should be accepted, but it must be PAID work. Someone who
is retired and sits on a Board or committee and is paid for this
work is not regarded as in paid work. Baby sitting, running a mail
order club etc IS regarded as paid work.*

13 Did you do any paid work in the 7 days ending Sunday
    last, either as an employee or as self-employed?
    Yes   1
    No   2

14 Which of these descriptions applies to your main activity
    in the last week, that is the seven days ending Sunday?
    Self-employed (full-time)   1
    Self-employed (part-time at least 10 hours per week)   2
    Full-time employment   3
    Part-time employment (at least 10 hours per week)   4
    Employment training   5
    Waiting to take up work   6
    Registered unemployed   7
    Unemployed but not registered   8
    Permanently sick or disabled   9
    Wholly retired from work   10
    Looking after the home   11
    At school/ full-time education   12
    Doing something else   13

BENEFITS

15 Do you <u>or any member of your household</u> receive at present any of the following state benefits? (Complete all items - if the answer is negative circle "No")

	Yes	No	Don't Know
(a) Job seekers allowance	1	2	3
(b) Income support	1	2	3
(c) One-parent benefit	1	2	3
(d) Family credit	1	2	3
(e) Housing benefit (rent rebate)	1	2	3
(f) Statutory sick pay/ sickness benefit	1	2	3
(g) Incapacity benefit	1	2	3
(h) Disability living allowance (65+)	1	2	3
(i) Widow's pension	1	2	3
(j) Attendance allowance(65+)	1	2	3
(k) Severe disablement allowance	1	2	3
(l) Child benefit	1	2	3
(m) State retirement pension	1	2	3
(n) Industrial injuries payment	1	2	3
(o) Invalid care allowance	1	2	3
(p) Other state benefits	1	2	3
(q) None of the above	1	2	3

SECTION D: INCOME

16 What is your own personal income before tax and national insurance contributions? Include all income from employment and benefits

£___,_____ . ___

17 **What period does this income relate to:**

Yearly	1
Monthly	2
Weekly	3
Fortnightly	4
Other (please specify)	5

18 **What is your total household income before tax and national insurance contributions? Include all income from employment and benefits**

£___,_____ . ___

19 **What period does this income relate to:**

Yearly	1
Monthly	2
Weekly	3
Fortnightly	4
Other (please specify)	5

SECTION E: RELIGION AND ETHNIC ORIGIN

20 **In terms of the two communities in Northern Ireland, are you considered by others to be:**

A member of the Catholic community	1
A member of the Protestant community	2
Other	3

SECTION F: DISABILITY

21 Do you have a long-standing illness disability or infirmity?

By long-standing I mean anything that has troubled you over a period of time or that is likely to affect you over a period of time?

Yes   1

No   2

22 If yes to Q21, to what extent does this disability affect your life?

Severe restriction eg on mobility/ unable to work/ leave the home	1
Considerable restriction eg unable to go out unaccompanied	2
Moderate restriction eg unable to drive	3
Mild restriction eg need to avoid certain areas/things	4
Other	5

SECTION G: HEALTH AND WELL BEING: SF-12

Now I would like to ask you some questions about your health.

23 In general would you say your health is...

Excellent	Very Good	Good	Fair	Poor
5	4.4	3.4	2	1

The following items are about activities you might do during a typical day. Does your health now limit you in these activities?

If so, how much?

24 Moderate activities, such as moving a table, pushing a vacuum cleaner, bowling, or playing golf:

Yes, limited a lot	Yes, limited a little	No, not limited at all
1	2	3

25 Climbing several flights of stairs

Yes, limited a lot	Yes, limited a little	No, not limited at all
1	2	3

During the past 4 weeks, have you had any of the following problems with your work or other regular daily activities as a result of your physical health?

26 Accomplished less than you would like

Yes   1

No   2

27 Were limited in the kind of work or other activities

Yes   1

No   2

During the past 4 weeks, have you had any of the following problems with your work or other regular daily activities as a result of any emotional problems (such as feeling depressed or anxious)?

28 Accomplished less than you would like

Yes   1

No   2

29 Didn't do work or other activities as carefully as usual

Yes   1

No   2

30 During the past 4 weeks, how much did pain interfere with your normal work (including both work outside the home and housework)?

Not at all	A little bit	Moderately	Quite a bit	Extremely
6	4.75	3.5	2.25	1

These questions are about how you feel and how things have been with you during the past 4 weeks. For each question, please give one answer that comes closest to the way you have been feeling.

How much of the time during the past 4 weeks:

	All the time	Most of the time	A good bit of the time	Some of the time	A little of the time	None of the time
31 Have you felt calm and peaceful?	6	5	4	3	2	1
32 Did you have a lot of energy?	6	5	4	3	2	1
33 Have you felt downhearted and depressed?	1	2	3	4	5	6

34 **During the past 4 weeks, how much of the time has your physical health or emotional problems interfered with your social activities (like visiting friends, relatives etc.)?**

All of the time	Most of the time	Some of the time	A little of the time	None of the time
1	2	3	4	5

35 **How true or false is each of the following statements for you?**

	Definitely True	Mostly True	Don't Know	Mostly False	Definitely False
I seem to get sick a little easier than other people	1	2	3	4	5
I am as healthy as anybody I know	1	2	3	4	5
I expect my health to get worse	1	2	3	4	5
My health is excellent	1	2	3	4	5

36 **If there is a change in your health over the past five to ten years what, in your opinion, caused this change? (Complete all items - if answer is negative circle "No")**

		Yes	No	No Response
(a)	Troubles related trauma: e.g. bombings, shootings, intimidation, attacks	1	2	3
(b)	Troubles related bereavement	1	2	3
(c)	Non-troubles related trauma: e.g. road accident, accident in the home	1	2	3
(d)	Non-troubles related bereavement	1	2	3
(e)	Occupational factors: stress, chemical pollution	1	2	3
(f)	Environmental factors: poor housing, lead pollution	1	2	3
(g)	Genetic disorder/progressive disease	1	2	3
(h)	Financial worries/shortages	1	2	3
(i)	Loss of job/unemployment	1	2	3
(j)	Isolation	1	2	3
(k)	Street disturbances	1	2	3
(l)	Military presence in my area	1	2	3
(m)	No change in health	1	2	3

SECTION H: EXPERIENCE OF THE TROUBLES

37 **How much experience would you say you have of the troubles?**

A lot	Quite a lot	Some	A little	Very little	None
1	2	3	4	5	6

Now, I would like to ask you some questions about specific experiences you may have had of the troubles. I have a list of experiences that people have had of the troubles, starting with common experiences.

38 Would you tell me how often, if at all, you have had the experience?

EVENT/EXPERIENCE	Every often	occasionally	seldom	never
(a) Hearing /reading news reports about troubles-related violence	1	2	3	4
(b) Getting caught in a bomb scare	1	2	3	4
(c) Straying into an area where I didn't feel safe	1	2	3	4
(d) Getting stopped and searched by the security forces	1	2	3	4
(e) Being stopped in a checkpoint	1	2	3	4
(f) Feeling unable to say what I think in a situation because of safety issues	1	2	3	4
(g) Being wary in the presence of people from the other community	1	2	3	4
(h) Having to take extra safety precautions to secure my home or workplace	1	2	3	4
(i) Having to change my normal routes,routines or habits because of safety	1	2	3	4

The next question deals with slightly more direct experience of the troubles.

39 Can I ask if you have had any of these experiences and if so how often?

EVENT/EXPERIENCE	Every often	occasionally	seldom	never
(a) Being called sectarian names *Interviewer: their definition of sectarian*	1	2	3	4

(b) Having to conceal things about myself -my name or addressbecause of safety	1	2	3	4
(c) Having to listen to my tradition being criticised or abused	1	2	3	4
(d) Feeling blamed or being blamed for the troubles	1	2	3	4
(e) Having to end friendships or having relationships disrupted because of the sectarian divide	1	2	3	4
(f) Having to turn down work opportunities because of troubles related danger	1	2	3	4
(g) Getting into physical fights about the troubles	1	2	3	4
(h) Having to avoid going into certain areas because of the troubles	1	2	3	4
(i) Having my schooling disrupted by the troubles	1	2	3	4
(j) Being forced to do things against my will	1	2	3	4
(k) Had experience of military organisations acting as punishment agencies	1	2	3	4
(l) Having to pay protection money to a paramilitary	1	2	3	4
(m) Being so afraid that I thought of leaving Northern Ireland	1	2	3	4

Now, I would like to ask about your work experiences.

(For interviewees with no work experience, go to Question 42)

40 Thinking about your current or last job, could you tell me which of the following best describes your workplace?

Mixed 50/50 workplace	1
Mixed, but more of my community	2
Mixed, but less of my community	3
Hardly mixed: very few of the other community	4
Not mixed: all of my community	5
Hardly mixed, very few of my community	6
Not mixed: all of the other community	7
Don't know	8

Intimidation at work

41 Did you have any of the following experiences at work in relation to the Troubles?

	Every often	occasionally	seldom	never
(a) Feeling uncomfortable with the attitudes or behaviour of colleagues from my own community	1	2	3	4
(b) Feeling confident that all of us were respected and safe, in spite of our differences	1	2	3	4
(c) Feeling outnumbered	1	2	3	4
(d) Feeling out of place and alienated by the atmosphere at work	1	2	3	4
(e) Feeling unsafe or threatened by some of the attitudes or events at work	1	2	3	4
(f) Feeling unsafe because of direct verbal threats made against me	1	2	3	4

		very often	occasionally	seldom	never
(g)	Feeling unsafe because of physical attacks on me or my property	1	2	3	4
(h)	Having to leave because of feeling unsafe or because of threats	1	2	3	4

The next question deals with some of the most severe, distressing and direct experience of the troubles.

42   Can I ask if you have had any of these experiences of the troubles and if so how often:

		very often	occasionally	seldom	never
(a)	Having my work place or business attacked	1	2	3	4
(b)	Having my workplace or business destroyed	1	2	3	4
(c)	Having my home attacked	1	2	3	4
(d)	Having to leave my home temporarily	1	2	3	4
(e)	Having to leave my home permanently	1	2	3	4
(f)	Having my home destroyed	1	2	3	4
(g)	Having my car hijacked/ stolen due to the troubles	1	2	3	4
(h)	Being close to a bomb explosiion	1	2	3	4

The next question deals with situations in the troubles where people have been injured or killed..

43   Can I ask if you have had any of these experiences and if so how often:

		Several times	More than once	Once	Never
(a)	Being caught up in a riot	1	2	3	4
(b)	Witnessing a shooting	1	2	3	4

(c)	Having a work colleague attacked	1	2	3	4
(d)	Having a work colleague killed	1	2	3	4
(e)	Having a neighbour attacked	1	2	3	4
(f)	Having a neighbour killed	1	2	3	4
(g)	Seeing people killed or or seriously injured	1	2	3	4
(h)	Having a close friend killed	1	2	3	4
(i)	Being physically attacked due to the troubles	1	2	3	4
(j)	Being injured in a bomb explosion	1	2	3	4
(k)	Being injured in a shooting	1	2	3	4
(l)	Having a member of my immediate family injured	1	2	3	4
(m)	Having a member of my immediate family killed	1	2	3	4
(n)	Having another relative injured	1	2	3	4
(o)	Having another relative killed	1	2	3	4

44 How much do you think each of the following are responsible for the troubles?

		Most Responsible	Responsible	Least Responsible	Don't Know
(a)	Republican paramilitaries in general	1	2	3	4
(b)	Loyalist paramilitaries in general	1	2	3	4

(c) The RUC	1	2	3	4
(d) The RIR/UDR	1	2	3	4
(e) The British Army	1	2	3	4
(f) Republican Politicians	1	2	3	4
(g) Loyalist Politicians	1	2	3	4
(h) British Politicians	1	2	3	4
(i) Irish Politicians	1	2	3	4
(j) All Politicians	1	2	3	4
(k) British Government	1	2	3	4
(l) Irish Government	1	2	3	4
(m) The Churches	1	2	3	4
(n) The silent majority in Northern Ireland	1	2	3	4
(o) People living in hard-line areas in N.I.	1	2	3	4

(p) Other, please specify ....

45 Indicate the extent to which the following periods of the troubles have affected you.

	Strong effect	moderate effect	slight effect	none	don't remember too young
(a) 1969 & the 1970's	1	2	3	4	5
(b) The 1980's	1	2	3	4	5
(c) The early 1990's	1	2	3	4	5
(d) 1994 to present day	1	2	3	4	5

46 To what extent have the following events in the troubles affected you?

	Affected me strongly	Moderately affected me	Affected me least	don't remember
(a) The civil rights campaigns	1	2	3	4

(b) Internment	1	2	3	4
(c) The Loyalist general strikes	1	2	3	4
(d) IRA bombing campaign	1	2	3	4
(e) Republican targeting of the RUC and security forces	1	2	3	4
(f) Feuds within republican paramilitaries	1	2	3	4
(g) Feuds within loyalist paramilitaries	1	2	3	4
(h) The hunger strikes	1	2	3	4
(i) Sectarian assassinations of Catholics by loyalist paramilitaries	1	2	3	4
(j) Sectarian assassinations of Protestants by republican paramilitaries	1	2	3	4
(k) Intimidation in housing	1	2	3	4
(l) Conflicts over parades and marching	1	2	3	4
(m) Punishment beatings and shootings by republicans	1	2	3	4

(n) Punishment beatings and shootings by loyalists	1	2	3	4
(o) The loyalist cease-fire	1	2	3	4
(p) The republican cease-fire	1	2	3	4
(q) Signing of the Anglo-Irish agreement	1	2	3	4
(r) The alleged shoot to kill policy of the RUC	1	2	3	4
(s) Loyalist bombings in the Republic of Ireland	1	2	3	4

SECTION I: EFFECTS OF THE TROUBLES ON YOU

Some people experience after-effects as a result of their experiences of the troubles. Can I ask you if you have had after-effects, for example:

	Frequently	Occasionally	Rarely	Never	Don't remember
47 Have you ever had a period of time when you kept having painful memories of your experience/s, even when you tried not to think about it?	1	2	3	4	5
48 Have you ever had a period of time when you had repeated dreams and nightmares about your experience/s?	1	2	3	4	5

112

49 Have you ever   1   2   3   4   5
    had a period of
    time when you
    you found your-
    self in a situation
    which made you feel
    as though it was
    all happening
    over again?

50 Have you ever   1   2   3   4   5
    had a period of
    time when you
    lost interest in
    activities that had
    meant a lot to
    you before?

51 Have you ever   1   2   3   4   5
    had a period of
    time when you
    were very jumpy or
    more easily startled
    than usual or felt
    that you had tobe on
    your guard all the time?

52 Have you ever   1   2   3   4   5
    had a period of
    time when you had
    more trouble than
    usual with sleeping
    due to your experiences
    in the troubles?

53 Have there ever   1   2   3   4   5
    been times when
    you felt ashamed or
    guilty about surviving
    events in the troubles?

54 **How recently have you had the symptoms described in Qs47-53?**

Within 6 months   1

6 months - 1 year   2

1 - 5 years   3

5 - 10 years   4

10+ years   5

No symptoms   6

55 **Approximately how long after the event/s did the symptoms described start?**

Within 6 months   1

6 months - 1 year   2

1 - 5 years   3

5 - 10 years   4

10+ years   5

No symptoms   6

Don't know   7

56 **Have the symptoms interfered in any way with your life?**

Yes, severe interference with my life   1

Yes, moderate interference with my life   2

In the past, but not in the present   3

Sometimes they affect me   4

No, they do not interfere with my life   5

No symptoms   6

SECTION J: MEDICATION

57 **Have you taken medication from any source - prescribed or nonprescribed - for any of these symptoms?**

Yes   1

No   2

If "No" go to Q60

58 **If yes, for how long have you take medication?**

Taken on one-off occasions/ single dose	1
One day or several days	2
Two weeks or less	3
2 weeks to a month	4
1 month - 1 year	5
1 - 5 years	6
More than 5 years	7
I am permanently on medication	8

59 **Please think only about tablets that you have been given to you because of the effects of the troubles on you. In your opinion, were these tablets given to you to: (Complete all items)**

	Yes	No
(a) Help you sleep	1	2
(b) To calm you down	1	2
(c) To give you a lift in mood	1	2
(d) To even out your moods	1	2
(e) To kill pain	1	2
(f) To keep away the memories	1	2
(g) To treat a physical condition	1	2
(h) Other	1	2

Self Medication with Alcohol/Drugs

60 **On balance, do you think your drinking has changed as a result of your experiences of the troubles?**

No, it has stayed the same	1
Yes, it has increased	2
Yes, it has decreased	3
I have always abstained	4
I abstain now	5

61   (a)   **Has there been a period of time when you drank a lot**
           after a particular experience of the troubles ?

           Yes   1

           No   2

     (b) If YES, for how long?

     Less than 6 months   1

     6 months - 1 year   2

     1 - 5 years   3

     More than 5 years   4

62   (i)   **If you have been taking medication or using alcohol**
           to help with the effects of the troubles, to what extent
           has this ever affected you?

     Severe interference with my life   1

     Moderate interference with my life   2

     Mild interference with my life   3

     No interference with my life   4

     Not applicable   5

62   **(ii) Has this medication or alcohol ever affected:**

		Affected me strongly	Moderately affected me	Affected me little	No Effect
(a)	your schooling, education or training	1	2	3	4
(b)	your home life, family relationships	1	2	3	4
(c)	your social life, hobbies & leisure	1	2	3	4
(d)	your other activities, such as driving	1	2	3	4

Now, I would like to ask about how the troubles may have affected
your health and well being.

63 Do you agree/ disagree that the troubles have :

	strongly agree	agree	neither agree nor disagree	disagree	strongly disagree
(a) Caused me a great deal of distress and emotional upset	1	2	3	4	5
(b) Made violence more a part of my life	1	2	3	4	5
(c) Made it difficult for me to trust people in general	1	2	3	4	5
(d) Left me feeling helpless	1	2	3	4	5
(e) Provoked strong feelings of rage in me	1	2	3	4	5
(f) Shattered my illusion that the world is a safe place	1	2	3	4	5
(g) Caused me not to want to have anything to do with the other community	1	2	3	4	5

Now I would like to ask how the troubles may have affected your family

64 Do you agree/ disagree that the troubles have:

	strongly agree	agree	neither agree nor disagree	disagree	strongly disagree
(a) Completely ruined my life	1	2	3	4	5
(b) Damaged my health	1	2	3	4	5
(c) Caused me to lose loved ones through death	1	2	3	4	5

(d) Physically damaged me/my family	1	2	3	4	5
(e) Severely altered the path my life would have taken	1	2	3	4	5
(f) Led to me/my family leaving our home through intimidation or fear of attack	1	2	3	4	5
(g) Influenced where I have chosen to live	1	2	3	4	5
(h) Caused me to worry a lot about rearing my children	1	2	3	4	5
(i) Made members of my family and/or me emigrate	1	2	3	4	5
(j) Made members of my family and/or me seriously consider emigration	1	2	3	4	5
(k) Divided members of my family against one another	1	2	3	4	5
(l) Made me extremely fearful for my own and my family's safety	1	2	3	4	5

Now I wish to ask how the troubles may have affected your life in terms of your education, work and income.

65   Do you agree/ disagree that the troubles have:

	strongly agree	agree	neither agree nor disagree	disagree	strongly disagree
(a) Seriously damaged my livelihood/ job/ business	1	2	3	4	5

(b)	Influenced the kind of work I do	1	2	3	4	5
(c)	Interrupted my educational opportunities	1	2	3	4	5
(d)	Restricted the number of areas I am prepared to go into for work	1	2	3	4	5
(e)	Led me to shop in certain areas/ businesses and not in others	1	2	3	4	5
(f)	Have created employment opportunities for me/members of my family	1	2	3	4	5
(g)	Caused damage or loss to my property	1	2	3	4	5

66 Would you agree or disagree that the troubles have affected your leisure pursuits in terms of restricting how and where you spend your leisure time?

Strongly agree	1
Agree	2
Neither agree nor disagree	3
Disagree	4
Strongly disagree	5

67 In general, would you agree/ disagree that the troubles have

		strongly agree	agree	neither agree nor disagree	disagree	strongly disagree
(a)	Nothing to do with me	1	2	3	4	5
(b)	Have not affected me very much at all	1	2	3	4	5

119

		strongly agree	agree	neither agree nor disagree	disagree	strongly disagree
(c)	Caused me a great deal of distress and upset	1	2	3	4	5
(d)	Severely impacted on the area I live in	1	2	3	4	5

Now I wish to ask how the troubles have affected your life in terms of the kind of person you are and how you present yourself.

68 Would you agree/ disagree that the troubles have:

		strongly agree	agree	neither agree nor disagree	disagree	strongly disagree
(a)	Led me to support activities that I would otherwise think wrong	1	2	3	4	5
(b)	Made me ashamed of being from Northern Ireland	1	2	3	4	5
(c)	Made me very careful about expressing an opinion in case I offend someone	1	2	3	4	5
(d)	Made me wary of letting people know details about my life	1	2	3	4	5
(e)	Made me bitter	1	2	3	4	5
(f)	Made me more understanding of other peoples' difficulties	1	2	3	4	5
(g)	Have taught me the pointlessness and dangers of wanting revenge	1	2	3	4	5
(h)	Led me to stick to the company of those from my own community	1	2	3	4	5

(i)	Caused me to question or lose my faith	1	2	3	4	5
(j)	Made me feel powerless to stop what was happening	1	2	3	4	5
(k)	Strengthened my faith	1	2	3	4	5
(l)	Led me to find a faith or religious beliefs I didn't have before	1	2	3	4	5
(m)	Made me angry with God	1	2	3	4	5

Now I wish to ask how the troubles may have affected your life in terms of your political attitudes?

69 Would you agree/ disagree that the troubles have:

		strongly agree	agree	neither agree nor disagree	disagree	strongly disagree
(a)	Shown those in power to be lacking in the will to sort this conflict out	1	2	3	4	5
(b)	Restricted my opportunities to get to know and understand people from the other community	1	2	3	4	5
(c)	Led to distrust politicians	1	2	3	4	5
(d)	Led me to avoid political discussions, and to keep my opinions to myself	1	2	3	4	5
(e)	Led me to have more negative feelings about the other community	1	2	3	4	5
(f)	Made me more determined to resist being pushed around politically	1	2	3	4	5

(g) Provoked me to great determination that things have to change and I will make contribution to bringing about that change	1	2	3	4	5
(h) Confirmed my belief about the mess made of this country by the older generation	1	2	3	4	5
(i) Shown dialogue and negotiation to be a dangerous waste of time	1	2	3	4	5

Now I would like to ask how the troubles have affected your life in terms of how you think about law and order.

70 Would you agree/ disagree that the troubles have :

	strongly agree	agree	neither agree nor disagree	disagree	strongly disagree
(a) Made me more critical of the police	1	2	3	4	5
(b) Made me believe more in the law and the court system	1	2	3	4	5
(c) Put paramilitaries in a position of having to police communities	1	2	3	4	5
(d) Has meant that many people who would not normally go to prison have been or are still in prison	1	2	3	4	5
(e) Made me feel sympathetic towards the police and the security forces	1	2	3	4	5

71 Overall how much do you think your experiences of the troubles have affected you?

Completely changed my life	1
Radically changed my life	2
Made some changes to my life	3
Made a small impact	4
Not at all	5

SECTION K: HELP & SUPPORT

72 Have you ever seen any of the following trained helpers about the effect of the troubles on you or on a member of your family?

		Yes	No
(a)	Psychiatrist	1	2
(b)	Clinical psychologist	1	2
(c)	GP and local doctor	1	2
(d)	Community nurse	1	2
(e)	Alternative health practitioner e.g. reflexologist, acupuncturist	1	2
(f)	Chemist/pharmacist	1	2
(g)	Social Worker	1	2
(h)	Child guidance	1	2
(i)	Support through School welfare/ educational psychologist	1	2
(j)	Teacher	1	2
(k)	Counsellor	1	2
(l)	Self help group	1	2
(m)	Marriage/relationship counsellor	1	2
(n)	Social Security Agency	1	2
(o)	Citizen's Advice Bureau	1	2
(p)	The Samaritans	1	2

(q)	Minister or priest	1	2
(r)	Faith healer	1	2
(s)	Lawyer or solicitor	1	2
(t)	Personnel department within my employment	1	2
(u)	Accountant	1	2
(v)	Local politician	1	2
(w)	Community worker	1	2
(x)	Other voluntary organisation	1	2

73 **Do you think the help available to you was satisfactory? (complete all items)**

		Yes	No	Not applicable
(a)	Yes, it was sympathetic & helpful	1	2	3
(b)	It was adequate only	1	2	3
(c)	It was insensitive	1	2	3
(d)	It was harmful	1	2	3
(e)	It was judgemental	1	2	3
(f)	It was critical of me	1	2	3
(g)	I couldn't find help	1	2	3
(h)	Did not need help	1	2	3

74 **Where, if from anywhere, did you receive the best help? (circle one only)**

Spouse	1
My children	2
Parents	3
Other close family	4
Close friends	5
Neighbours	6
Work colleagues	7
Those in a similar position to myself	8
My local Doctor	9

Psychiatrist	10
Clinical psychologist	11
Community nurse	12
Alternative health practitioner e.g. reflexologist, acupuncturist	13
Chemist/pharmacist	14
Social Worker	15
Child guidance	16
Support through School welfare/ educational psychologist	17
Teacher	18
Counsellor	19
Self help group	20
Marriage/relationship counsellor	21
Social Security Agency	22
Citizen's Advice Bureau	23
The Samaritans	24
Minister or priest	25
Faith healer	26
Lawyer or solicitor	27
Personnel department within my employment	28
Accountant	29
I received appropriate help from no-one	30

75 **If you found if difficult to get help, was this mainly because...**

I didn't know where to look for help	1
I was unable to find help that met my needs satisfactorily	2
I was not able to look for help	3
I did not believe that anything could help me at that time	4
Other (please specify)	5

SECTION L: COMPENSATION

As you may know, the Northern Ireland office pays compensation to people injured or who have sustained a loss in the troubles.

76 Have you ever received such compensation from the Northern Ireland office?

Yes	1
No	2

If yes...

77 Do you think the compensation was enough?

Yes	1
No	2

78 What problems, if any are you aware of with the compensation system?

(a)	Doesn't give enough money	1
(b)	It is not fair: it gives some people more than others for the same injury	2
(c)	Delays in payments cause financial problems to businesses	3
(d)	There is no appeal against the amount granted	4
(e)	I was asked a lot of very intrusive questions	5
(f)	Not aware of any problems	6
(g)	Other (please specify)..	

SECTION M: LEGAL REDRESS

79 Do you agree/ disagree that the law does enough to deal
    with the effects of the troubles on people?

	strongly agree	agree	neither agree nor disagree	disagree	strongly disagree
(a) Yes, the law does enough	1	2	3	4	5
(b) No, stiffer sentences are required for those who kill and injure people	1	2	3	4	5
(c) No, not enough effort to catch those responsible	1	2	3	4	5
(d) No, the law does not protect innocent people	1	2	3	4	5
(e) No, the law victimises people further	1	2	3	4	5
(f) No, there are two laws, one for us and one for them	1	2	3	4	5
(g) I have no faith in the law here	1	2	3	4	5
(h) The law is not suited to dealing with the troubles - something else is needed	1	2	3	4	5

Interviewer briefing

*I would like to thank you for your time and can assure you that
all information will be treated in total confidence.*

*Would you like information about self-help and support
organisations in your area?*

Thank you for your co-operation.

This questionnaire includes the SF-12 Health Survey, item numbers 23 to 34 in
this questionnaire. Reproduced with permission of the Medical Outcomes
Trust, Copyright 1994 The Health Institute; New England Medical Centre

Appendix 2
The collection of the qualitative data

In all over 70 interviews were conducted by the end of the project. Since interviews were perceived to have a useful function for some interviewees, we continue to have requests to interview people. Some people feel the need to "tell their story" or have their story acknowledged by someone in a semi-official position, and we have, in part, filled some of this need for some people. However, at the point we designed the questionnaire, not all interviews had been conducted, therefore we will describe the position at the point when the questionnaire was being designed.

The Qualitative Data: The In-Depth Interviews
We embarked on a series of in-depth interviews with a cross section of people throughout Northern Ireland, which were to serve a number of functions. First, they were to provide qualitative data on the range and diversity of people's experience of the Troubles. Second, they were to provide subjective assessments of the effects of the Troubles on the range of people interviewed. Third, they were to form the basis for the questionnaire design, which was to be used in the survey.

In Northern Ireland, "people affected by the Troubles" is not a homogenous group: people have been affected in different ways and have different needs as a result. To collect detailed qualitative illustrations of the diversity and range of experience and needs of those affected by the Troubles, we conducted sixty-three in-depth interviews with men and women, old and young, Catholic and Protestant from various parts of Northern Ireland. These interviews provide a wide variety of personal stories of experiences in the Troubles.

Selection of interviewees
In selecting interviewees, we avoided using the personal contacts of the researchers. We chose instead to use the contacts and suggestions from a range of people, some of whom were working in this field, and some were not. We asked them to

nominate people that they thought should be interviewed, in order to achieve the goal of collecting a cross section of experiences of the Troubles. With the help our own Board of Directors, other self-help groups, organisations and key individuals throughout Northern Ireland we recruited a group of interviewees from both communities, genders and a range of income groups. Towards the end, people were asked to nominate certain categories of people, such as men over 60, or Protestants from rural areas, who seemed not to be represented in our matrix. We used the database on deaths as a guide to the kind of religious and urban-rural balance we wished to achieve, since the Troubles have disproportionately affected certain groups, and we wanted to reflect this in our qualitative data collection.

Once nominated, letters and information leaflets were sent to all the voluntary groups and individuals involved in nominating interviewees. They were informed about the work of this study and asked to identify individuals suitable for in-depth interview. In these leaflets, we explained who we were, the purpose of the study, the way we handled consent and confidentiality. We offered people who were willing to participate in an interview the opportunity to tell their own story and be listened to carefully and respectfully.

Generally, this recruitment strategy was successful, although in the end, some organisations did not nominate anyone for interview. This appeared to be for organisational reasons, rather than any reluctance to co-operate. Only one organisation approached -an organisation for Loyalist prisoners - did not wish to co-operate, because they said that they were involved in doing their own research. Several organisations approached, did not respond in spite of several reminders, and it is difficult to interpret this: possible explanations are the overburdened nature of many organisations in this field, or a lack of trust in us as a research project. Some organisations that co-operated presented us with other problems. One organisation, who nominated its employees for interview, seemed to us to have briefed their nominated interviewees before we interviewed them, and we got a "party line" in response from all their nominated interviewees.

These biased responses reduced the usefulness of the data considerably.

Whilst no set of interviews is going to be complete, we can clearly identify some gaps in the data that we failed to fill. In spite of several attempts through various channels to set up interviews with soldiers' families, or former soldiers, we did not succeed in obtaining interviews from this cohort. Conversely, in some areas where we were interviewing, people referred themselves for interview, they wanted to tell their stories. In these circumstances, we conducted the interview, even though we had not sought it. We took the view the research and the researchers were committed to being responsive to the communities and individuals that we were working with. This happened in the case of four interviews out of the sixty-five we had conducted at this point. It is interesting to note that none of these interviews added any significantly new material to our data set. In all, we conducted eighty five in-depth interviews.

We closely monitored the spread of interviewees, bearing in mind the need to allow for our own biases in the selection of interviewees. Tables 1.1 and 1.2 show how we set about this. Thirty-seven Catholics, twenty-five Protestants and one "other" were interviewed, thirty-seven of whom were males and twenty-six were female. Twenty-two people from Belfast, fourteen from Derry Londonderry, were interviewed and fifteen from small towns, four from rural areas, three from border regions and five from London.

Table 3.37: Age/gender/religion/location matrix of interviewees for in-depth interviews

	Age 16-20		Age 21-40		Age 41-60		Age 61-80		Total
	male	female	male	female	male	female	male	female	
Catholic	0	2	11	3	7	10	2	2	37
Protestant	0	0	5	1	8	6	4	1	25
Other	0	0	0	0	0	1	0	0	1
Total	0	2	16	4	15	17	6	3	63
Location									
Belfast	0	1	5	1	2	7	5	1	22
Derry	0	0	2	2	6	3	0	1	14
Small town	0	0	3	1	3	6	1	1	15
Rural	0	0	0	0	3	1	0	0	4
Border	0	1	2	0	0	0	0	0	3
London	0	0	4	0	1	0	0	0	5
Total	0	2	16	4	15	17	6	3	63
Class									
Professional	0	1	8	1	6	5	3		25
Skilled Manual	0	0	3	1	6	2	0	0	12
Unskilled Manual	0	1	0	0	0	1	0	0	2
Long term Unemployed/ benefits	0	0	5	2	3	9	3	2	24
Total	0	2	16	4	15	17	6	3	63

In terms of socio-economic class, twenty-five people interviewed were classified as professional, twelve were skilled manual workers, two were unskilled manual workers and twenty-four people were either on benefits or were long-term unemployed. Table 3.37 shows the numbers interviewed in each category: gender, age, location and employment status.

The most sensitive balance in the qualitative data collection was the balance between the two main traditions in Northern Ireland. We were anxious that the spread of our qualitative data roughly corresponded with the spread of the experience of the Troubles in the general population. The ratio of Catholics to Protestants interviewed was compared with the ratio of Catholics and Protestants killed in the Troubles. The ratio of Catholic to Protestant interviews was 37 Catholic to 25 Protestant, a ratio of 1: 0.68. We wished to compare this to the ratio of Catholics to Protestants killed, using the death rate by religion. However, as can be seen in the following table, there is a wide variety in ratios, depending on how the death rate is calculated.

Table 3.38: Ratio of Catholic to Protestant deaths in the Troubles as a base for monitoring the number of in-depth interviews: projected number of interviews shown in brackets.

	Calculated from 1991 census		Calculated from average of 1971, 1981 and 1991 census	
	Catholic	Protestant	Catholic	Protestant
Civilians only	2.48	1.46	3.01	1.26
	(37)	(21)	(37)	(15)
Civilians & security forces	2.5	1.9	3.1	1.6
	(37)	(28)	(37)	(19)
Excluding deaths caused by paramilitaries in own community	1.9	1.6	2.3	1.4
	(37)	(31)	(37)	(22)

Since we included security forces in our interviews, and since we did not exclude those Catholics bereaved or affected by Republican violence and those Protestants bereaved or injured by Loyalist violence, the appropriate ratios are the "civilians + security forces" ratios. The most accurate ratio is one calculated on an average of the 1971, 1981 and 1991 census population figures, which suggests that if we interview 37 Catholics, the appropriate number of Protestants to interview would be 19. We actually interviewed 25 Protestants, as can be seen in the previous tables, since we wished to achieve a better overall spread of data, and properly include Protestant experience. Given the overall balance of population in Northern Ireland[1] and our aim to include the experience of those who had relatively little experience of the Troubles, we felt this was justified.

Procedures used in qualitative data collection and management

Interviews were conducted by the Research Officer and the Project Director, both of whom are trained interviewers. Interviewees were provided with information about where to go

---

[1] Out of a total population of 1,577,836 at the 1991 census, 605,639 (38.4%) were Catholic, 675,688 (42.8%) were Protestant and a further 296,509 (18.8%) gave other responses, stated that they had no religion or did not state a religion.

for advice and help, apprised of voluntary groups that exist for people affected by the troubles, and given a leaflet on self-help where appropriate. Interviews were tape-recorded to broadcast quality. Each interview lasted approximately two and a half hours, and interviews ranged from fifty minutes to four hours in duration.

Consent

Before the tape recording began, the issue of consent was discussed with the interviewees. Each interviewee was asked to complete a consent form on which was a written undertaking of confidentiality and anonymity. However, some interviewees wished their names to be used. The signing of the form signified that the interviewer was satisfied that the interviewee understood and accepted the process taking place. This form asked interviewees to indicate with a tick:

(a) that they agree to be interviewed,

(b) that they are aware the interview is tape recorded and

(c) that they will be sent a full transcript of the interview and have the chance to make any changes to the transcript before it can be used in the research.

The interviewees were also given an undertaking that they will be shown the final version of the text of their interview before it was published and they will be consulted about photographs or images put alongside their interview in any publication or exhibition. This issue of confidentiality was regarded as a very important issue and the interviewees were guaranteed complete confidentiality. However, interviewees were also given the option of having their names used in any publication and some chose this option. By signing the consent form, interviewees acknowledged that they had been fully informed about the interviews and that they had been given information leaflets and a contact telephone number for The Cost of the Troubles Study. The interviewer also signed the form as a witness on behalf of The Cost of the Troubles Study. The interview data is not analysed or referred to in detail here, but was used to inform the design of the questionnaire, as we shall see later. However, the interview data was used to prepare other publications and at each stage we went back to interviewees to obtain consent, as we were anxious not to increase our informants' sense of vulnerability. A small but significant number of interviewees withdrew their consent at various stages in this process. When this happened, the person's wishes were immediately respected without question, and we made no attempt to dissuade them from their decision. Those interviews, where they had taken place, were not used in the research.

Structure of interviews

Interviews were semi-structured, in that interviewers, having ascertained certain demographic facts about the interviewee, namely age group, gender, marital status, location and perceived politico-religious identification, asked three basic questions. Interviewees were asked, "What is your experience of the Troubles?" Interviewees were shown a time-line, indicating birth, childhood, teenage years and present age, and asked to review their entire experience in the light of the time-line. Interviewees were then asked, "How do you think the Troubles have affected you?" although some of the effects of the Troubles may have already emerged in the answer to the first question. On both these questions, interviewees were prompted to answer broadly, not just the most traumatic experiences of the Troubles, but early experiences, not just the emotional effects, but the financial, educational, attitudinal effects also. Finally, interviewees were asked how they imagine their lives would have been different if the Troubles had not taken place. In retrospect, this last question was not as useful (or crucial) as the first two, and a significant number of interviewees had difficulty in answering it.

Distress in interviews

We anticipated that some interviewees would become distressed in the course of interviews, and put in place arrangements for linking interviewees with supportive services should the need arise, as detailed elsewhere. Otherwise, the response made to distress on the part of the interviewee was simply to listen sympathetically, and remain with the interviewee until they had recovered some degree of equilibrium. About mid-way through conducting the interviews, it became clear that some interviewees, particularly those who were living with considerable emotional effects of the Troubles, found the process of being interviewed useful in some way. Some interviewees reported this to us, and associates of interviewees approached us wishing to be interviewed. We had also anticipated that the interviews would be distressing to the interviewers, and this proved to be the case. Formal and informal debriefing of interviewers formed part of the project work, as discussed elsewhere. Nonetheless, both interviewers report lasting effects from conducting the interviews.

Confidentiality and anonymity

Standard practices of confidentiality and anonymity had to be amended to ensure that the interviewees identity was concealed, in cases where they wished it to be concealed. In some cases, interviewees divulged information that would be legally or morally impossible to publish, such as naming people allegedly involved in acts of violence who had never been convicted. In such cases we negotiated with the interviewee so that we did not end up holding such information. The agreed interview transcript was then coded for NUD.IST[2] analysis, and a selection of interviews were edited into "poems" which were then used in our exhibition, "Do You Know What's Happened?" which has toured a number of venues. Other issues arose in the collection of qualitative data, which will be dealt with in more depth in other publications.

Processing the qualitative data

All interviews were transcribed, and after consents had been obtained, were coded for NUD.IST analysis. A fuller report on the interview data processing and analysis will be provided elsewhere. For the purposes of this publication, we will limit our discussion to the way the data informed the design of the questionnaire.

---

[2] NUD.IST is a computer software package for use in analysing qualitative data.

Appendix 3

NUD.IST coding tree for interview data

(1)   **experiences:**
(1 1)   **self**
(1 1 1)   injured
(1 1 2)   hijacked
(1 1 3)   partner's death
(1 1 4)   son ,daughter injured
(1 1 5)   dead son, daughter
(1 1 6)   injured sibling
(1 1 7)   dead sibling
(1 1 8)   extended family injury
(1 1 9)   dead extended family
(1 1 10)   other people I know injured
(1 1 11)   other people I know dead
(1 1 12)   self assaulted
(1 1 14)   been in premises when bombed
(1 1 15)   bystander in bomb explosion
(1 1 16)   directly involved in shooting incident
(1 1 17)   bystander in shooting incident
(1 1 18)   house raids in my home
(1 1 19)   have been arrested
(1 1 20)   have been in prison
(1 1 21)   family member imprisoned
(1 1 22)   have received threats
(1 1 23)   have lost my home in the Troubles
(1 1 24)   have been victim of workplace intimidation
(1 1 26)   have been caught up in rioting
(1 1 28)   have been made to do something against will
(1 1 29)   have been in bomb scare
(1 1 30)   have been involved in helping family members in
             such sitations
(1 1 31)   Involved in legitimate politics
(1 1 32)   verbal abuse by 'other side'
(1 1 33)   involved in community action
(1 1 34)   involved in paramilitary
(1 1 35)   victim of discrimination

(1 1 36)   victim of harassment
(1 1 37)   upset by distress of close family members friends
(1 1 38)   aware of cultural difference
(1 1 39)   unaware of culture of other community
(1 1 40)   have been invovled in identifying dead body
(1 1 41)   lived in mixed area
(1 1 42)   victim of punishment beatings
(1 1 43)   live in an enclave area
(1 1 44)   been victim of harassment outside Northern Ireland
(1 1 45)   death of father or mother in Troubles
(1 1 46)   suffered abuse or harassment by own side
(1 1 47)   had direct negative experience with Orange Order
(1 2) neighbours
(1 2 2)   death of neighbours
(1 2 3)   physical assault of neighbours
(1 2 4)   neighbours bombed
(1 2 8)   house raids on neighbours
(1 2 11)   neighbours threatened
(1 2 12)   neighbours lost home
(1 3) immediate family
(1 3 1)   injured
(1 3 2)   death of immediate family member
(1 3 3)   physical assault of immediate family member
(1 3 4)   immediate family in premises which were bombed
(1 3 5)   immediate family bystander at bomb
(1 3 6)   directly involved in shooting incident
(1 3 7)   bystander at shooting incident
(1 3 8)   immediate family had house raids on home
(1 3 9)   immediate family being imprisoned
(1 3 10)   immediate family being arrested
(1 3 12)   immediate family lost their home
(1 3 15)   immediate family involved or caught up in riot
(1 3 18)   distress or psychological disturbance to immediate
              family
(1 3 19)   immediate family had to identify dead body
(1 3 20)   immediate family involved in paramilitary
(1 3 21)   affected political opinions of immediate family
(1 3 22)   punishment beatings of immediate family

(1 4) extended family
(1 4 1)   injured
(1 4 2)   dead
(1 4 3)   physical assault on extended family
(1 4 4)   extended family bombed
(1 4 6)   extended family involved in shooting
(1 4 9)   extended family arrested
(1 4 10)   extended family imprisoned
(1 4 15)   extended family involved in riot
(1 4 18)   extended family had to identify body
(1 4 19)   distress or psychological disturbance of extended
                  family
(1 5) friends
(1 5 1)   friends injured
(1 5 2)   friends dead
(1 5 3)   friends assaulted
(1 5 6)   friends involved in shooting
(1 5 10)   friends imprisoned
(1 5 11)   friends had threats made to them
(1 5 13)   friends had workplace intimidation
(2) effects of the troubles
(2 1) social
(2 1 1)   restricted my social circle
(2 1 2)   made me isolated, lonely
(2 1 3)   I do not go out
(2 1 4)   Troubles has improved social circle
(2 1 5)   felt my identity changed
(2 2) economic
(2 2 1)   lost income
(2 2 2)   got into debt
(2 2 4)   lost my career
(2 2 5)   got no compensation for losses
(2 2 6)   got compensation for losses
(2 3) political
(2 3 1)   given me hatred of other side
(2 3 2)   made me anti-violence
(2 3 3)   made me support violence
(2 3 4)   makes me blame British Government
(2 3 5)   makes me blame politicians

(2 3 6)   makes me respect other tradition
(2 3 7)   makes me feel that others do not want to listen
(2 3 8)   gives me sympathy for politicians
(2 3 9)   interviewee offers solution
(2 3 10)   points out advantages of peace
(2 4) emotional effects
(2 4 1)   fear
(2 4 2)   grief
(2 4 3)   rage
(2 4 4)   hatred
(2 4 5)   depression
(2 4 6)   hopelessness
(2 4 7)   powerlessness
(2 4 8)   guilt
(2 4 9)   devastation
(2 4 10)   anger
(2 4 11)   need to blame
(2 4 12)   bitterness
(2 4 14)   jealousy
(2 4 15)   bitterness towards 'other side'
(2 4 16)   stunned
(2 4 17)   forgiveness
(2 4 18)   personal growth
(2 4 19)   sadness
(2 4 20)   other
(2 4 22)   worry
(2 4 23)   feel need to give strong protection of children
(2 4 24)   suspicious of others
(2 4 25)   I can't talk about it
(2 4 26)   bewildered and confused
(2 4 27)   strong feelings about perpetrators
(2 5) migratory
(2 5 1)   I wish to leave
(2 5 2)   I have left
(2 5 4)   I am committed to stay
(2 5 5)   I left and came back
(2 5 6)   went for holiday break
(2 6) psychological
(2 6 1)   intrusions

(2 6 2)   panic attacks
(2 6 3)   lost memory
(2 6 5)   numbing
(2 6 6)   survivor guilt
(2 6 7)   avoidance
(2 6 8)   denial
(2 6 9)   vulnerable
(2 6 10)   shaking
(2 6 11)   sleep problems
(2 6 12)   nervous breakdown or nerves
(2 6 13)   deep shock
(2 6 14)   suicidal
(2 6 15)   nightmares
(2 6 16)   flashbacks
(2 6 17)   other

(2 7) educational
(2 7 1)   education interrupted
(2 7 2)   created educational opportunity
(2 7 3)   deepened understanding
(2 7 4)   restricted understanding
(2 7 5)   educated in a one sided way

(2 8) health
(2 8 1)   chronic pain
(2 8 2)   hair loss
(2 8 3)   weight loss
(2 8 4)   ulcers
(2 8 6)   asthma
(2 8 7)   intestinal problems
(2 8 10)   physical disability
(2 8 11)   diabetes
(2 8 12)   other

(2 9) community
(2 9 1)   increased polarisation and distance
(2 9 2)   tokenism in relation to cross community
(2 9 3)   commitment to cross community work
(2 9 5)   cynicism and distrust of authorities
(2 9 6)   militarisation of local area
(2 9 7)   community trauma
(2 9 8)   family division

(2 9 9)   the issue of parades/marching season
(2 9 10)   community tension
(4) demographics
(4 1) age
(4 1 1)   15-17
(4 1 2)   18-20
(4 1 3)   21-24
(4 1 4)   25-30
(4 1 5)   31-40
(4 1 6)   41-50
(4 1 7)   51-60
(4 1 8)   61-70
(4 1 9)   71-80
(4 2) gender
(4 2 1)   male
(4 2 2)   female
(4 3) religion
(4 3 1)   Protestant
(4 3 2)   Catholic
(4 3 3)   other
(4 4) urban rural
(4 4 1)   Belfast
(4 4 2)   Derry Londonderry
(4 4 3)   town
(4 4 4)   rural
(4 4 5)   London
(4 7) marital status
(4 7 1)   single
(4 7 2)   married
(4 7 3)   separated
(4 7 4)   divorced
(4 7 7)   widowed
(5) Help Received
(5 1)   Personal
(5 1 1)   my children
(5 1· 2)   parents
(5 1 3)   other close family
(5 1 4)   neighbours
(5 1 5)   friends

(5 2) Medical
(5 2 1)   Local GP
(5 2 2)   Psychiatrist
(5 2 3)   psychiatric nurse
(5 2 4)   psychiatric institution
(5 3)   Other-Formal
(5 3 1)   Social worker
(5 3 5)   Counsellor
(5 3 8)   Probation Officer
(5 4)   Other-Informal
(5 4 1)   CAB
(5 4 3)   Church
(5 4 8)   Self Help Groups
(5 5)   Other Coping Strategies
(5 5 2)   Creative writing and art classes
(5 6)   No Help
(6) coping measures
(6 1)   short term prescribed drugs
(6 2)   prescribed drugs long term
(6 3)   short term non prescribed drugs
(6 5)   crisis use of alcohol
(6 6)   long term alcohol use
(6 11)   religion
(6 12)   refused to take any drugs
(6 13)   enrolled in courses
(6 14)   talking in your own organisation
(6 15)   work helped me cope
(6 16)   hobbies helped me cope
(6 17)   forming groups or organisations helped me cope
(7) Media
(7 1)   anger at media
(7 2)   media intrusion
(7 4)   media bias
(7 7)   being manipulated by the media
(7 8)   using media
(8) Security Forces
(8 1)   awareness of security forces
(8 2)   experience with security forces
(8 3)   harassment by security forces

(8 4)   breaking of sexual boundaries by security forces
(8 5)   physical attack by security forces
(8 6)   lack of help
(8 7)   afraid to call security forces
(8 8)   anger and blame at security forces
(8 9)   manipulation of evidence
(8 10)   refusal to co-operate
(8 11)   sympathy for security forces
(8 13)   harassment outside Northern Ireland
(9) Story analysis
(9 1)   trouble free past
(9 2)   class division before 1969
(9 3)   class division after 1969
(9 4)   I am not a bigot
(9 5)   I have been guilty of "innocent sectarian"

Appendix 4

Table 3.39 Severity of experience of the Troubles by Severity of Effect in High Intensity Locations

Experience Of the Troubles		Effects of the Troubles					Total
		complete change	radical change	some change	small impact	not at all	
A lot	Count	39	20	49	10	2	120
	% within experience	32.50%	16.70%	40.80%	8.30%	1.70%	100.00%
	% within effect	48.10%	40.00%	25.30%	8.90%	8.70%	26.10%
Quite a lot	Count	36	22	60	13	2	133
	% within experience	27.10%	16.50%	5.10%	9.80%	1.50%	100.00%
	% within effect	44.40%	44.00%	30.90%	11.60%	8.70%	28.90%
Some	Count	3	8	63	36	1	111
	% within experience	2.70%	7.20%	56.80%	32.40%	0.90%	100.00%
	% within effect	3.70%	16.00%	32.50%	32.10%	4.30%	24.10%
A little	Count	1		13	27	6	47
	% within experience	2.10%		27.70%	57.40%	12.80%	100.00%
	% within effect	1.20%		6.70%	24.10%	26.10%	10.20%
Very Little	Count	1		9	26	10	46
	% within experience	2.20%		19.60%	56.50%	21.70%	100.00%
	% within effect	1.20%		4.60%	23.20%	43.50%	10.00%
None	Count	1				2	3
	% within experience	33.30%				66.70%	100.00%
	% within effect	1.20%				8.70%	0.70%
Total	Count	81	50	194	112	23	460
	% within experience	17.60%	10.90%	42.20%	24.30%	5.00%	100.00%

Table 3.40 Severity of experience of the Troubles by Severity of Effect in Medium Intensity Locations

Experience Of the Troubles		Effects of the Troubles					
		complete change	radical change	some change	small impact	not at all	Total
A lot	Count	7	12	25	9	3	56
	% within experience	12.50%	21.40%	44.60%	16.10%	5.40%	100.00%
	% within effect	58.30%	28.60%	12.60%	5.40%	6.70%	12.00%
Quite a lot	Count	2	11	48	17		78
	% within experience	2.60%	14.10%	61.50%	21.80%		100.00%
	% within effect	16.70%	26.20%	24.10%	10.10%		16.70%
Some	Count	3	10	66	47	12	138
	% within experience	2.20%	7.20%	a47.80%	34.10%	8.70%	100.00%
	% within effect	25.00%	23.80%	33.20%	28.00%	26.70%	29.60%
A little	Count		5	37	36	5	83
	% within experience		6.00%	44.60%	43.40%	6.00%	100.00%
	% within effect		11.90%	18.60%	21.40%	11.10%	17.80%
Very Little	Count		4	22	48	20	94
	% within experience		4.30%	23.40%	51.10%	21.30%	100.00%
	% within effect		9.50%	11.10%	28.60%	44.40%	20.20%
None	Count			1	11	5	17
	% within experience			5.90%	64.70%	29.40%	100.00%
	% within effect			0.50%	6.50%	11.10%	3.60%
Total	Count	12	42	199	168	45	466
	% within experience	2.60%	9.00%	42.70%	36.10%	9.70%	100.00%
	% within effect	100%	100%	100%	100%	100%	100%

Table 3.41 Severity of experience of the Troubles by Severity of Effect in Low Intensity Locations

Experience Of the Troubles		Effects of the Troubles					
		complete change	radical change	some change	small impact	not at all	Total
A lot	Count	3	5	13	1		22
	% within experience	50.00%	22.70%	59.10%	4.50%		100.00%
	% within effect	50.00%	20.80%	10.70%	0.50%		5.60%
Quite a lot	Count	3	2	24	13	3	45
	% within experience	6.70%	4.40%	53.30%	28.90%	6.70%	100.00%
	% within effect	50.00%	8.30%	19.80%	7.00%	5.60%	11.50%
Some	Count		11	45	44	4	104
	% within experience		10.60%	43.30%	42.30%	3.80%	100.00%
	% within effect		45.80%	37.20%	23.80%	7.40%	26.70%
A little	Count		2	17	40	7	66
	% within experience		3.00%	25.80%	60.60%	10.60%	100.00%
	% within effect		8.30%	14.00%	21.60%	13.00%	16.90%
Very Little	Count		4	22	80	31	137
	% within experience		2.90%	16.10%	58.40%	22.60%	100.00%
	% within effect		16.70%	18.20%	43.20%	57.40%	35.10
None	Count				7	9	16
	% within experience				43.80%	56.30%	100.00%
	% within effect				3.80%	16.70%	4.10%
Total	Count	6	24	121	185	54	390
	% within experience	1.50%	6.20%	31.00%	47.40%	13.80%	100.00%
	% within effect	100%	100%	100%	100%	100%	100%

Table 3.42 Help received by location: have you ever seen any of the following...

Source of help/ obtained	High intensity Number (%)		Medium intensity Number (%)		Low intensity Number (%)	
	Yes	No	Yes	No	Yes	No
Psychiatrist	45	394	11	453	7	391
	(10.3)	(89.7)	(2.4)	(97.6)	(1.8)	(98.2)
Clinical psychologist	14	422	2	464	2	396
	(3.2)	(96.8)	(.4)	(99.6)	(.5)	(99.5)
GP/ local doctor	171	272	57	410	40	360
	(38.6)	(61.4)	(12.2)	(87.8)	(10)	(90)
Community nurse	67	370	2	463	8	389
	(15.3)	(84.7)	(.4)	(99.6)	(2)	(98)
Alternative health	10	427	0	465	0	398
practitioner	(2.3)	(97.7)	(0)	(100)	(0)	(100)
Chemist	137	302	23	442	14	385
	(31.2)	(68.8)	(4.9)	(95.1)	(3.5)	(96.5)
Social worker	46	391	3	462	2	396
	(10.5)	(89.5)	(.6)	(99.4)	(.5)	(95.5)
Child guidance	10	424	0	465	0	398
	(2.3)	(97.7)	(0)	(100)	(0)	(100)
School welfare/ educational	16	419	1	463	0	398
psychologist	(3.7)	(96.3)	(.2)	(99.8)	(0)	(100)
Teacher	37	398	2	463	2	396
	(8.5)	(91.5)	(.4)	(99.6)	(.5)	(99.5)
Counsellor	23	412	7	458	6	392
	(5.3)	(94.7)	(1.5)	(98.5)	(1.5)	(98.5)
Self-help group	40	396	3	462	4	394
	(9.2)	(90.8)	(.6)	(99.4)	(1)	(99)
Marriage counsellor	3	433	2	463	0	398
	(.7)	(99.3)	(.4)	(99.6)	(0)	(100)
Social security agency	104	333	3	462	1	397
	(23.8)	(76.2)	(.6)	(99.4)	(.3)	(99.7)
Citizens advice bureau	64	372	7	458	3	395
	(14.7)	(85.3)	(1.5)	(98.5)	(.8)	(99.2)
Samaritans	2	434	3	462	1	397
	(.5)	(99.5)	(.6)	(99.4)	(.3)	(99.7)
Minister or priest	70	367	26	439	20	379
	(16)	(84)	(5.6)	(94.4)	(5)	(95)
Faith healer	3	432	4	459	1	394
	(.7)	(99.3)	(.9)	(99.1)	(.3)	(99.7)
Lawyer or solicitor	90	346	30	434	15	380
	(20.6)	(79.4)	(6.5)	(93.5)	(3.8)	(96.2)
Personnel at work	13	423	2	461	1	394
	(3)	(97)	(.4)	(99.6)	(.3)	(99.7)
Accountant	3	433	1	461	0	395
	(.7)	(99.3)	(.2)	(99.8)	(0)	(100)
Local politician	117	318	15	446	14	381
	(26.9)	(73.1)	(3.3)	(96.7)	(3.5)	(96.5)
Community worker	115	322	6	455	9	386
	(26.3)	(73.7)	(1.3)	(98.7)	(2.3)	(97.7)
Other voluntary organisation	92	344	3	460	5	389
	(21.1)	(78.9)	(.6)	(99.4)	(1.3)	(98.7)

Table 3.43 Sources of best help by location
Source of best help

Table 3.12 Have you ever taken medication from any source?

		Highest Intensity	Middle Intensity	Least Intensity	Total
Spouse	Count	90	32	29	151
	% within source	59.60	21.19	19.21	100.00
	% within Location	24.13	16.16	9.35	17.14
Children	Count	17	5	9	31
	% within source	54.84	16.13	29.03	100.00
	% within Location	4.56	2.53	2.90	3.52
Parents	Count	76	18	28	122
	% within source	62.30	14.75	22.95	100.00
	% within Location	20.38	9.09	9.03	13.85
Other close family	Count	65	2	17	103
	% within source	63.11	20.39	16.50	100.00
	% within Location	17.43	10.61	5.48	11.69
Close friends	Count	22	8	11	41
	% within source	53.66	19.51	26.83	100.00
	% within Location	5.90	4.04	3.55	4.65
Neighbours	Count	1	7		8
	% within source	12.50	87.50		100.00
	% within Location	0.27	3.54		0.91
Work colleagues	Count		2	1	3
	% within source	66.67	33.33		100.00
	% within Location	1.01	0.32	0.34	
Those in similar position	Count	6	3	9	18
	% within source	33.33	16.67	50.00	100.00
	% within Location	1.61	1.52	2.90	2.04
Local doctor	Count	12	7	1	20
	% within source	60.00	35.00	5.00	100.00
	% within Location	3.22	3.54	0.32	2.27

Table 3.43 Sources of best help by location
Source of best help

Table 3.12 Have you ever taken medication from any source?

		Highest Intensity	Middle Intensity	Least Intensity	Total
Psychiatrist	Count	3	2	1	6
	% within source	50.00	33.33	16.67	100.00
	% within Location	0.80	1.01	0.32	0.68
Alternative health practitioner	Count	1			1
	% within source	100.00			100.00
	% within Location	0.27			0.11
Chemist	Coun		1		1
	% within source		100		100
	% within Location		0.51		0.11
Social worker	Count	1			1
	% within source	100			100
	% within Location	0.27			0.11
School welfare/ educational psychologist	Count	1			1
	% within source	100			100
	% within Location	0.27			0.11
Teacher	Count			1	1
	% within source			100	100
	% within Location			0.32	0.11
Counsellor	Count		3	1	4
	% within source		75	25	100
	% within Location		1.52	0.32	0.45
Self help group	Count	1			1
	% within source	100			100
	% within Location	0.27			0.11
CAB	Count	1			1
	% within source	100			100
	% within Location	0.27			0.11

Table 3.43 Sources of best help by location
Source of best help

Table 3.12 Have you ever taken medication from any source?

		Highest Intensity	Middle Intensity	Least Intensity	Total
Minister/priest	Count	7	3	2	12
	% within source	58.33	25.00	16.67	100.00
	% within Location	1.88	1.52	0.65	1.36
Lawyer/solicitor	Count	3	3		6
	% within source	50	50		100
	% within Location	0.80	1.52		0.68
Personnel Dept in my job Count	Count	1			1
	% within sourve	100			100
	% within Location	0.27			0.11
received appropriate help from no-one	Count	65	83	200	348
	% within source	18.68	23.85	57.47	100.00
	% within Location	17.43	41.92	64.52	39.50
Total	Count	373	198	310	881
	% within source	42.34	22.47	35.19	100.00
	% within Location	100	100	100	100

Appendix 5

Excerpts from in-depth interview data

Sleep disturbance

The interview data illustrated the kinds of difficulties people had with sleeping as a result of the Troubles. One interviewee said:

> Sleep was really, it was very hard to sleep. And when I did sleep it was all bad, nightmares and very very bad dreams. Woke up in sweats.

Another interviewee reported similar difficulties:

> ...Nerves and I can't go out anymore because the fear never leaves you. I'll always get nightmares. I still get nightmares to this day. And I waken up and I waken the whole house with the roaring you do. Because when you sleep everything just flashed back in front of you.

Yet another reported:

> I repeatedly had dreams about [...] Street, it became a real fear for me, we had to get from the town to R...ville going up [...] street and there is one pocket in it where that pub was and I would have nightmares about, just an awful panic about getting past that part of that street from the corner half way up it, and when I get up near the top of the road then I sort of calm down again. I can actually in my dreams feel my heart going and panic setting in. I would have had that year after year every now and again.

Use of prescribed medication

One interviewee reported:

> My doctor, being very kind, gave me some little tranquillisers and sleeping tablets, the sleeping tablets I think I used for about three months because I wouldn't have shut an eye otherwise and then I stopped because I thought well I don't want to become addicted to them. The tranquillisers I must have had for anything up to five years because I only took them on a very bad day, you know, I would have taken half of one.

Others were less fortunate, and became addicted

> I've had different tablets, and the doctor in hospitals have
> given me, I attend and they reckon they give me a nights
> sleep, but I can't sleep. He gave me a different tablet but I
> had to go off those because they made me all itchy. And I
> wish I could get off them. Twenty five years is a long time
> to be on tranquillisers. But I know there is an awful lot
> on them because of different things happen them over
> through the troubles.

One respondent reported speech and memory difficulties
which were attributed to drug use:

> I would put that down to drugs. I've seen me saying things
> and words are coming out in the wrong order. And you
> know it is happening. Writing a word down, you write it
> down and the spelling is correct and yet would say to Jess
> "Spell that word." And recall, remembering somebody's
> name. It was almost embarrassing so I devised a method to
> cope with that. I simply walked up to people and said "We
> met yesterday but give me your name again." You used to
> try and bluff your way and say through the conversation
> I'll pick up the person's name, or I'll pick up where I seen
> them but memory is affected and I think that blame it on
> drugs. I could be right, I could be wrong, I don't know.

A further interviewee reported parenting difficulties, again
attributed to drug use:

> They lost me for seventeen years, eighteen years down the
> line. You know Marie, they didn't have a mother. 'Cause
> I was only a figure sitting there for to be used - to give them
> money. I was there for that. That was the only reason. I
> wasn't their mother. My mother was their mother. I
> wasn't their mother at all. Do you know what I mean?
> And I was just a figure sitting in a chair. Not that any of
> them abused me, not that I can remember that any of
> them abused me. But on saying that, they should have
> shot me dead with [my husband], for I was dead anyway
> for those seventeen years with tablets.

Alcohol

Interviewees reported a range of experiences with alcohol. Some drink for a limited period after a bereavement:

> Because I got awful depressed and I cried and cried and cried. And funny enough after my sister - her like - whenever she was killed it was drink I went to. I mean, I started drinking even in the house - what I never done. But then it was my son that said the me, "Every time I come in here you're drinking you're drinking!" And then it just sort of way sunk in it wasn't doing no good anyway. So then I just stopped it

Others developed more long-standing problems with alcohol, subsequent to a traumatic experience in the Troubles:

> I certainly, at the time, blamed the traumatic incident for the next six month's apparent dramatic, spinning out of control of my drinking to the point where I couldn't do anything at all but drink, never mind do things with drink. I, realising, realising that things had got to a point that I could not conceive how I could continue to live without drink.

Another interviewee reported a similar experience after an experience in the Troubles:

> I was drinking very heavily, and I mean every day. You are talking seven days a week.

Interviewees evaluated the effectiveness of alcohol as a coping strategy. One interviewee said:

> I think they used drink as an excuse to bury themselves in deeper down, and the drink just made things worse, because you thought it was helping you at the time. You sort of like though, we'll I'll just go down and sit and have a drink, so you get yourself into such a bad habit. And you get yourself into such a bad way of living.

Another interviewee described the effect on his nervous symptoms acquired as a result of Troubles related trauma:

> The drink would stop it for me up until the first half a

dozen pints. And then anybody that's ever had a drink problem will tell you it then magnifies it after that. And all the things that you are trying to get away from just get bigger. And then when you 're drunk, the frustration seems to get braver and wants to show its face. And it comes out and it 's the people that are closest to you that suffer then because your abuse is directed at them, although they did nothing to deserve it. But that 's who ends up being the brunt of it.

Impact on family life/ anxiety about family

One interviewee reported:

I mean all I do now is live on my nerves. That's all I live on is just nerves. Nerves and wondering what's going to happen next. And are my sons going to be all right, or whether I'm going to get a wrap at the door, am I going to get a phone call about him? To tell me that he's dead somewhere. Or whatever it is they're going to do, I don't know. That's just the way I live. I just live in constant worry. That's all I have is constant worry. I would never get rid of my worry I don't think.

Bereavement and loss

One interviewee described the effect of the Troubles thus:

What the Troubles meant to me, the Troubles meant to me that it has lost, well it has divided a community, it has destroyed families, it has taken away friends of mine who were literally murdered. And it has taken neighbours away, it has seen people locked up, all the bad things...

Another interviewee multiply bereaved in the Troubles said:

The Troubles has taken over my whole life. It has been my whole life.

Financial loss

One interviewee described his experience of damage to his business:

To repair damage caused by vandals between £300 and £1200 per annum. Two years ago I spent £65000 on refurbishment but still the defacing of the property continues. You know you are losing money but it is accepted as a war situation, so it becomes a matter of keeping the show on the road to save your own self-respect. Sectarian louts continuously damage my commercial property. Weekly they damage the stone and wooden surrounds at the front of the shop by sticks, bricks and this week one was using a golf club to damage the plaster below one of the windows. The night the new door went on, it was scored with Stanley knives or screwdrivers. Three external spouting systems were removed within four weeks. Eggs and stones are thrown regularly at the shop sign and windows. The door and walls are covered in slogans. I know this is the work of a gang no more than twenty in number and it does cause me annoyance, but balancing them are thousands of decent Catholics and their support more than makes up the financial loss. The most I paid for one night's damage was £900, last October I paid £200 for one night's damage, so annually for the past odd twenty years between £400 and £1,500.

Punishment beating

Another described his experience of punishment beatings and what he sees as the impact on his educational attainment:

The paramilitary beatings that I got spoilt everything for me. The beatings have spoilt everything. I can't read and I can't write. I lost everything because of that. I was doing all right at school. But when that came, that was when I left school. I was in school one day maybe out of 4 months because of them'uns and like you couldn't turn round and say to the school that paramilitaries are going to come to my family. You have to watch what you say to people.

Overall impact

One interviewee described the impact of the Troubles on her:

I come from a loving relationship, two beautiful children, a wonderful husband, a friend and everything was brilliant. Although we had our ups and downs with the

RUC and the house raids, but we sort of tried to overlook that and not let it take hold of our relationship. And then all of a sudden, no daddy. Another child and I hated them, later. About two years after and I would have been very angry with them.

Who is responsible?

One interviewee described a common attitude to politicians:

You feel that you are being hustled and that you are a pawn in somebody else's game. Politicians don't really take peoples fears and needs into account and it seems that a very very small group are in the driving seat. I think that is very unfair.

A second interviewee said:

Politicians didn't seem to be making any progress. It seemed to me that they were just making things worse almost daily, so I felt that there was some real need for somebody to get out there and try and do something positive to improve relations rather than just to antagonise people.

One interviewee described attitudes to the security forces:

Part-time UDR officers would have been under attack as well, not because of their work but because of their part-time activities and I always thought that was very unfair. They were just trying to do their job and I didn't think it was right. Equally I thought the same about the British Army and that they were only doing their job as well. It wasn't their battle and they were being brought in and I thought they were very badly treated.

Sources of help

One interviewer described her experiences of help:

My boy would have been very violent in the house after his father died. And he would have been kicking out and kicking doors and he'd have been hitting me and he's just been doing a lot of things. I went to get him seen to. I went to a family unit at the hospital, the child development clinic. There was a social worker, health visitor, psychiatrist, child psychologist. There was a few people there and there was a two-way screen and I was speaking with someone, one of the team members. They observed the family and I had put my case, what was happening in the house and where there was a breakdown and that. It was my last resort because I just couldn't take no more of his behaviour problems. And rather than him go to the sessions I used to go myself and I used to relay what was happening in the house.

Another interviewee reported:

I suffered from depression, it's just I would get very down. Now at the minute thank goodness I don't feel so bad. But I have been through very bad times. I've been on different tablets from the doctor and that. I've a very, very good doctor. I've had her about ten years now, she's a lady doctor and she's very, very understanding you know.

One interviewee, widowed in the Troubles described her experience of help within her family:

I'd a great daughter. I would start work from 8.30 in the morning and about 2.30/2.45 went to the pub, got the drink and a taxi home. My daughter ran my house and signed the pension books and whatever. She ran my house at 14. She has been so supportive, she had been my crutch in more ways than one. Even yet she would be. But at that time, that child must have been in some hell of a state she had to see this and put up with it and there was nothing she could do about it.

Another interviewee described her family experience of getting help:

My mummy didn't get any help really either, other than from the neighbours. After the initial shock and the doctors and all left, that was it, you were left to cope. Other than the neighbours calling in, that was all the help we got. No one came near us.

Yet another interviewee describes the situation for those

bereaved in the early Troubles:

> Well it in those days there was no such thing as WAVE [a voluntary organisation offering help for those affected by the Troubles] or anything. You just went to the doctors or psychiatrist or the day hospital or were on tablets. I'm still on sleeping tablets. I'm not a very good sleeper. But there was nowhere that you could go and speak to people who had been through it although unfortunately there was a few friends of mine that had lost their husbands and sons. We just kept in touch with each other.

Another interviewee describes the impact of the lack of help on her:

> I remember actually at times thinking, "I am going out of my mind" you know, when you were going through really bad stages. You were coping through the daytime but maybe at night, having nightmares, when I would be alone thinking, "Oh my God, I'm going crazy, I'm really going crazy with grief', and yet I didn't know where to turn to. My doctor, being very kind, gave me some little tranquillisers and sleeping tablets. The sleeping tablets I think I used for about three months because I wouldn't have shut an eye otherwise and then I stopped because I thought well I don't want to become addicted to them. The tranquillisers I must have had for anything up to five years because I only took them on a very bad day, you know, I would have taken half of one.

Compensation

One interviewee described his experience of the compensation system:

> I think, well I think that I was still, I think it was still the Northern Ireland government, I'll just think, I'm nearly sure about that and I remember when I, when I got offered me £500. It was a fair bit of money but even then it was ridiculous. I said no way. So I got another one for £750 when the case was going to court and I went up into the court that day. I was still on crutches because of the injuries in my leg. I couldn't even straighten my leg, you

know the skin was healing and this boy came out to me and I says I'm not taking that there and he went away and when he came back he said, "Look a thousand quid." I said, "What, you're joking." He said I advise you strongly to take it and I'm saying to the wife, "What should I do?" She stops and she says to me. "I don't know!" And we haggled and haggled and then in the end I said, "Aye." And the minute I said, "Aye," I could've cut my tongue out. It was just the feeling I had at that time. I took the thousand pound and I tell you I was sick after it.

Notes

Notes

Notes